GRAND PRIX MEN

GRAND PRIX MEN

TED MACAULEY

ANDRE DEUTSCH

First published in Great Britain in 1998
By André Deutsch Limited
76 Dean Street
London W1V 5HA
www.vci.co.uk

André Deutsch is a VCI plc company

ISBN 0 233 99422 X

Typeset by Derek Doyle & Associates
Mold, Flintshire.
Printed by in the UK by MPG Books Ltd,
Bodmin, Cornwall

1 3 5 7 9 10 8 6 4 2

Ted Macauley's previous books include:

Hailwood, Cassell, 1968
Mike the Bike Again, Cassell, 1980
Mike, Buchan & Enright, 1984
Yamaha, Cadagon Books, 1979
Revised Edition, 1983

CONTENTS

To Dinky Dee

FOREWORD BY BERNIE ECCLESTONE

Chief Executive of Formula One Administration Ltd, Vice-President of FIA in charge of Promotional Affairs

Grand Prix Men . . . Ted Macauley has been one for as long as I have known him. That means that he and I, each in our own different way, share a common goal – to bring Formula One to the focus of the world at large and show it for the fabulous spectacle it is to the 450 million people, in more than 130 countries, who regularly watch it on television.

As with every major sporting occasion, the Olympics, the Football World Cup, the Americas Cup, the Derby, there is an army of people who put their efforts into ensuring the success of the event – and Formula One, with sixteen races a season, is no different.

Those of us deeply involved rarely have time to stop and think about what we are doing because we are so engrossed in the day-to-tday demands that Formula One imposes. But, here, Ted Macauley has taken the time to look behind the scenes, to talk at length to myself and other Grand Prix Men, whose lives and interests are bound by an enthusiasm to get the show on the road.

It is a unique and totally different look at Formula One, from a perspective that will give outsiders an insight into the workings, the moods, the emotions and the opinions of the men behind the drivers. But the stars are here too, the guys whose highly paid job it is to make the cars perform to everybody's expectations, including their own.

Books of this depth are few and far between in Formula One and if it achievese its aim, and opens up a world that can be a mystery to thsoe outside the paddock, then it will have done our sport a great service.

I hope you enjoy it.

MIKE CHAPMAN
Benetton Physiotherapist

He sat, sweating profusely in his T-shirt and blue shorts, gazing out of the darkened window of the Benetton motorhome onto Monaco's busy harbour. Out there celebrity laden speedboats scurried between the ocean going cruisers of the rich and beautiful. Stockport, he confessed, felt a long way off . . .

Mike Chapman's job is to care for and monitor the fitness and well being of Benetton's two drivers, the Italian Giancarlo Fisichella, and his Austrian teammate Alexander Wurz. The fitness of the drivers is a vital element in the structure of any team serious about winning races and titles, a point once made by Michael Schumacher, who said: 'You can have the greatest, fastest, best-handling car in the business but if you are not fit enough to cope with its capabilities and you don't have the stamina to stay with it, then you might as well be driving a supermarket trolley.'

Chapman's physical training skills were honed in the Royal Marines, an environment where individual control and self-sufficiency stem from the confidence inherent in good health and high levels of fitness. One of the parallels between the Marines and Formula One is that both demand tremendously high levels of precision and dedication. Nowadays, drivers are as strong and flexible as top-class athletes, their physical development is due to the individual training programmes thought up for them by Chapman and his ilk.

The role of the physio is crucial as few athletes in any branch of sport are forced to absorb as much physical strain and mental stress as a grand prix driver. 'The G-forces alone would kill your grandmother,' said Nigel Mansell, the 1992 world champion. Even though he was bullishly strong, Mansell frequently finished races on the point of exhaustion.

Michael Schumacher is widely regarded as the fittest man on the circuit. After one particularly gruelling race Damon Hill sat dehydrated, sweating and ashen with effort alongside the German. Schumacher looked as if he had undergone nothing more strenuous than a refreshing shower. 'Just look at him,' Damon said as he reached out and touched the brow of a coolly smiling and serene Schumacher, 'there's not a drop of sweat on him. He must be bloody Superman.'

Schumacher's superior fitness gives him an edge over his rivals and it is indicative of the German's dedication is his fitness programme, which includes a daily workout on an exercise bicycle. His aim is to boost his normally resting pulse rate of 50 beats per minute to 140 bpm and keep it that way for an hour. His average pulse rate when in the car is 120 bpm but he works to 140 bpm in training because during stressful moments in a race it will soar to 160 bpm. The preparation means that his body is able to cope with such demands because it has been forewarned.

In a sport where the smallest of details can make a substantial difference to a race's outcome, a race driver must put his heart and soul into his fitness campaign. Once in the cockpit of a car travelling at 200 mph a driver is in for a torrid time with G-forces that will increase the weight of his head and helmet by a factor of five. The race, and every corner, will load tremendous pressures on to him, and the demands on reflexes, endurance, eyesight, concentration, the neck muscles and reserves of sheer strength are unrelenting.

Alexander Wurz thought he was fit when he joined Benetton, but, under Chapman's guidance, he soon realized there was yet another plateau to reach. 'If drivers are not at an absolute peak,' says Wurz, 'they will end up exhausted, fall out of the car at the end of the race and suffer the sort of hallucinations that have them seeing crocodiles on the circuit.'

Wurz recalled a time when he drove in an International GT championship race at Suzuka in Japan. 'The temperatures were up to 40F in the shade,' he said. 'The humidity was 100 per cent and the in-car temperature was a steady 75F. That would have been bad enough and hard to cope with during a normal grand prix race of about an hour and a half, but we had to keep going for four-and-a-half hours. I dehydrated so badly I lost three kilos in weight and it was the worst experience I have ever had in a race car. I felt terrible when it was all over. I reckon I only survived what was one hell of battering to the end because I was so fit and I have carried that requirement into Formula One.

'It is important to have good endurance levels and to be able to withstand mental stresses that can wear you out just as quickly as the physical demands. Secondly, you have to be fit and strong in all the right areas for the job.'

Racing drivers need to concentrate on the neck, shoulders, arms and back because the strain of the G-forces, between G-4 and G-6, really tests a driver's capability to withstand stresses that a jet fighter-pilot doesn't have to cope with for the same length of time. The head is in the airstream and the neck takes the brunt of the buffeting that is inevitable when braking, when travelling over jarring bumps, and at every corner of every lap. And there is no let up.

The rest of the body has little more respite. When travelling at high speeds there may be centrifugal forces at work that will induce spinal compression and make it hard to breathe, for instance at curves like the awesome Eau Rouge at Spa in Belgium. Turning the steering wheel can be the equivalent of lifting a 20 kg weight. Fingers, knees, ankles, wrists and elbows suffer a non-stop barrage around a cramped cockpit. While the six-point safety harness limits problems caused by movement it creates others. If the driver is uncomfortable or his overalls or fireproof underwear is pinching he is stuck with it until the end of the race. This once happened to Eddie Irvine in 1997 in Brazil. Whilst driving a spare car that had been set up for Schumacher, his harness somehow worked its way between his legs and left him in agony but unable to remedy the problem, unless he surrendered precious time in a pit stop, or pulled out of the race. Neither option was acceptable so Irvine kept going even though he could barely walk away from the car at the finish.

Dehydration is another serious concern. As much as a litre of body fluid can be lost in a race mainly from the blood system because the driver cannot perspire freely in the fireproof overalls. This can result in fatigue and, therefore, lack of concentration. Peripheral vision can deteriorate and perspective suffer distortion as blood flow to the eyes is impaired, especially when braking heavily and in high-speed, high G-force turns where lateral loading on the neck muscles reaches pressures in excess of 30 kg. It is a problem that can be compounded on bumpy tracks such as Interlagos in Brazil and around the Buenos Aires circuit in Argentina where some corners are driven virtually blind.

Wurz pinpoints circuits like Silverstone, one of the fastest on the F1 calendar, as a typical test of strength. 'It's really quite quick and there are major G-forces to cope with up to around G-4,' he says. 'When you are going round a corner like Club, your head suddenly weighs about 40–45 kg and it feels like your neck muscles are supporting two big buckets full of water. And, it is important to remember, it is not just once, it is all the time, without a break, on every corner for sixty or seventy laps.'

Chapman's pedigree as a physical training instructor in the Royal Marines qualified him perfectly for the task of getting the two Benetton drivers to the required level of fitness and keeping them there. He joined the Marines straight from school, staying with the physical training wing for ten years before qualifying as a chartered physiotherapist. In 1990 he quit the Forces and moved to Exmouth in Devon, where he took up a position in the National Health Service, working for GPs in fund-holding practices. 'But,' says Chapman, 'I never lost my enthusiasm for my first love, sport. And I was heavily involved in sports medicine and in coaching boxing, football, gymnastics, rugby, the lot. I aligned myself with just about every local sports club I could find and then worked through the summer for television as physio on ITV's *Survival of the Fittest* programme. In between times I was amassing an array of qualifications and doing a lot of postgraduate study in sports medicine.'

Chapman's career path then took an unusual turn. In 1991 he joined Exeter City Football Club, a lowly team struggling under the managership of Alan Ball, England's 1966 World Cup hero.

'I saw an advert in my local paper,' explained Chapman, 'So I rang them up, spoke to Alan Ball, and I got the job. And for seven years I was the guy who used to run on the pitch with the old sponge and cold water treatment for an injured player. But, of course, it was a lot more complex than that and there was much more to the job of keeping a football team up to scratch.

'I made them eat properly and gave them a diet of the right things – pastas and plenty of carbohydrates – and insisted that it wasn't enough just to have the ability to play. I drove it home to them that it didn't stop there and absolute fitness was essential, not only so that they could shake off injuries quicker, but because it gave them an edge. There were lessons on those late-night, long-distance bus journeys with footballers that I have carried with me into Formula One. But then all athletes and grand prix drivers come into that category – are linked by the same fundamental needs – if they want to succeed rather than just take part.'

Chapman's eventual switch from football to Formula One came through a surprise telephone call to his treatment room at the Exeter City training ground: 'It was a guy I hadn't seen for seven years, since I had left the Marines, Bernie Shrosbree, a triathlete. I used to look after him on *Survival of the Fittest* and I knew his reputation as one hell of a competitor on the world triathlon circuit. We had developed a bond, a shared empathy, which you don't lose how ever long it is before you see each other again.

'Then I received this telephone call from him at work right out of the blue. He had been the fitness adviser to the Subaru world rally team and when David Richards, the Benetton boss, moved to take over the Formula One team and wanted to set up a human performance centre, Bernie was put in charge of the plan. David's idea was to oversee and assess driver fitness in a laboratory under clinical conditions and give them appropriate training regimes and help them with physiotherapy. That's where I came in.

'Bernie remembered what I had done for him and what my skills were and offered me a contract. What the team used to do before was sub-contract people like me on a daily or event basis but the idea had now gone deeper. And with the new performance centre at the Benetton headquarters at Oxford they wanted to initiate a corporate facility for all the employees and not just the drivers and the Formula One race team staff, but a system to benefit the entire company. They wanted to promote the health and well being and general fitness of all the employees.

'The more I heard about it, the more I fancied the job. And I agreed to go testing in Barcelona on a sub-contracting basis to see what it was like, to let them see what I was like and what I could do and it didn't take me long to realize that if I was going to have a change of direction in my career this might be just what I'd been waiting for.

'I didn't know the first thing about racing and, hand on heart, I had only ever seen it on television but if there was football on the other channel I'd switch over. It wasn't that I wasn't interested, it just wasn't my passion – that was soccer. But since I became involved full-time before the 1998 season started it has grown on me and I can see how people fall for its magic.

'But the real fascination is the undercurrent of activity, all the action behind the scenes and away from the glare and focus of public attention. The effort that goes into getting a driver onto that stage for the big show is awesome and there's an army of people all working to one end, sometimes until three and four in the morning, and thinking nothing of the sort of fourteen-hour working days that would send a union shop steward into fits.'

When Chapman first became a part of Formula One he had no pre-conceived notions about what the drivers would be like. 'That would have been far too arrogant of me,' he says. 'After all, I was the newcomer in their sport. It was up to me to learn even though I was coming in as a teacher. It's like any professional sport, you can be a bloody good doctor or a brilliant physio or technician and you can arrive at a football club or any other top-flight set-up with more qualifications than you can count, but until you find out how it all works and what the demands and needs are at all levels you would be foolish to try and stamp your authority too quickly.'

Chapman's first move was to look at information assembled by Professor Syd Watkins, the Formula One medical chief, and other material put together by universities and various medical experts all over the world. 'We wanted to examine all the information available to us on resting pulse rates, how the heart rate accelerates at certain stress points in races, how the respiratory system operates and whether a driver hyperventilates or holds his breath while the G-forces affect him in a really long and demanding corner. The trouble is, if they are holding their breath for a long time it could be dangerous because it can cause a temporary loss of concentration.'

Despite the secrecy that often surrounds Formula One Chapman is happy to explain some of the ideas Benetton are putting into operation. 'If you are looking for simple remedies, ways to help a driver on the really difficult corners, the long ones which are the hardest to cope with physically at speed and under severe G-forces, we get them to do basic things like trickle breathe [breathing out slowly and gradually so the pressure is kept low]. It's a state of mind, really, and a lot of drivers are aware of it; but it's my job to make them realize it, understand it, and try and promote the solutions.

'There's still an awful lot of research to be done in this field and it will reward everybody. We will use the lab at Oxford to test drivers for cardio responses, and we'll undertake VO2Max examinations [ratio of oxygen taken into the body versus oxygen into blood] for respiratory benefits and look into body fats, blood flow, dexterity skills and any other aspect of physical stress.

'When it comes to driving a race car, you are dealing with static strength at high G-forces, especially in cornering. So the neck, shoulders and upper back have all got to be able to counteract the immense stresses put on them. Reflexes, of course, have to be sharp. Dexterity, hand-to-eye co-ordination, and focus and attention levels are paramount when you are fast approaching the blackout condition because of the loading on your faculties and your body on a long bend.

'Don't forget, not only are they racing, competing and challenging other drivers at speed and under conditions that would floor most of us mere mortals, they are having to concentrate intensely all the time on the feedback from the pits and what's happening on the readouts. The mental pressure is enormously demanding so they have to be highly tuned.'

Chapman is full of praise for the discipline of the two drivers under his charge. 'My two guys, Alexander and Giancarlo, are in good shape. They are lean because they carefully watch their diets and follow the advice they are given because they understand it is for their own good and it gives them a better chance of winning.'

Diet has a crucial bearing on the life of a Formula One driver and weight, of course, is a vital issue in the struggle to gain a micro-second's advantage. A racing driver generally weighs around 65 kg and carries virtually no fat on his lightly but well-defined muscular body. He will consume only 2,000–4,000 calories a day. Meals have to be high in essential but complex carbohydrates, but as low as possible in fats because a fat-heavy meal will adversely affect blood circulation, a factor that can be critical in a sport where the heart rate moves up and down the scale so dramatically.

A race driver's daily intake over the four days at a grand prix will start with a breakfast consisting of something like muesli or porridge with sliced banana and grated apple, washed down with honey-sweetened weak tea. He will then have a mid-morning snack of fruit, accompanied by litres of mineral water. This will see him through to dinner when he can have a bowl of vegetable soup, a piece of wholemeal bread without butter, a plate of pasta with low-fat sauce, steamed broccoli, yoghurt, dried fruit and nuts and fruit juice or mineral water. This may be followed by a corn and soya cake. Red meat, Sunday roasts, juicy steaks and racks of lamb are banned. So is junk food (despite Jacques Villeneuve's passion for it), sugar, any food that contains fat, and alcohol. An egg is considered to be a once-a-week treat.

Chapman's painstaking preparation for his Benetton role was undertaken with a study of both his drivers' personalities so he knew what to expect from each of them and how to deal with their needs. 'Alexander is extremely meticulous and he needs to plan everything well ahead so he knows exactly what he should be doing and where he should be at any given time,' says Chapman. 'He is relaxed, but extremely astute and with a well-developed sense of responsibility, particularly in one so young. He is very organized. He likes to know his day and what it holds. He plans it down to the finest detail and if he has to be at an engineers' meeting, say for 9.15 a.m., he will arrive at the circuit at 8.30 a.m. so he can have a bowl of muesli and be up there twenty minutes before they need him because he is really focused.

'Alex likes a lot of time on his own, so before a race I make sure that he is quiet and undisturbed so that he can concentrate. He can sit down, relax and chill out without the likes of me pestering him but I make sure he knows I am there if he needs me. Then there'll be a little knock at my door and he'll come in and we'll do what we need to do: a chat or a massage or some treatment. We just play it as it goes and deal with problems as they arise without making any we don't want.

'Giancarlo is a more passionate sort of guy with rather more immediate reactions and a less regimented attitude to life. Generally, he lets everything swim over him and takes it all in his stride and is wonderfully relaxed and at ease. He likes me to give him a physical checkover. Where they are similar is that they are both fastidiously conscientious when it comes to fitness. And they get on really well, they are good friends and team-mates.'

When Chapman describes his role with Benetton it becomes clear that no detail is too small in the world of Formula One. 'A typical day for me, when I have my contact with them both, can vary depending on where we are and the logistics involved,' he says. 'But the first thing I do when I get to a grand prix is make sure there are some gymnasium facilities we may use, and then touch base with both the drivers.

'I normally stay in the same hotel as them, so the marketing department at Benetton arrange for me to travel and be ahead of them either by a day or a few hours, so that I can check out the suitability of the fitness facilities either on site or in the local area. I contact the boys when they arrive to make sure they are OK, they haven't suffered any injuries or setbacks or have any problems that I can sort out and that they are fit and well. It's better, I feel, to get any problems resolved sooner rather than later and to work on them right away. So, communication with the drivers is the first essential.

'Then I get along to the circuit, set up the motorhome treatment area and organize a rest place for Alexander and Giancarlo and make sure that everything I need to keep them in tip-top shape is on stream. I like them to arrive at the circuit and find that everything they expect for their well-being and comfort is in place. I liaise with the truckies for all their clothing to be delivered and got ready so that when they arrive they feel comfortable and easy straight away in a nice relaxed atmosphere.

'If the room was a mess, which it never is because I wouldn't allow it, it wouldn't worry either one of them because they are both so easy-going and helpful and they would understand and still co-operate.

'The medical room in the team motorhome has all the supplies I need to remedy the less severe bangs and strains and bruises they suffer, like the twisted ankle and wrist I had to put right when Giancarlo fell over playing football in a charity match with Schumacher.'

Of course, no matter how fit the drivers are they are not immune to injury. But their superior fitness means that they do not stay injured for as long as you might think, as Chapman explains. 'Giancarlo had a road car crash on his way to Imola for the San Marino Grand Prix, another crash in the race and a major shunt in testing in Barcelona. So it was a pretty painful and miserable ten days for the boy but because he is so fit, like most of them, his ability to recover is really good. The rule is simple: the fitter you are and the more careful you are with what you eat and drink, the better the healing processes.

'Of course, there are freaks of nature: people like George Best, the footballer, who seemed to be able to eat everything and drink as much booze as he liked and abuse his body with late nights and yet could still play football like it was a dream sequence. But then the life-threatening demands placed on a grand prix driver when he goes to work don't lend themselves to that sort of lifestyle, how ever attractive it might appear to be.

'The penalties for disregarding your own safety are too severe and irreversible in this game. One blink at the wrong time, one fleeting failure of concentration, and you could be dead. Or, worse, somebody else could be.

'Giancarlo was reminded very sharply of the dangers that can threaten even the super-fit and the most aware and alert of drivers when he had his shunt and hit the wall extremely hard in Barcelona. He was quite shaken up and was taken to the circuit hospital for a complete checkover.

'He was in there for about three quarters of an hour for observation and I got him back after that; happily there were no signs of any problems but I stayed with him at the hotel all night and kept checking on him at regular intervals.

'The next morning I gave him a thorough examination and reckoned it was safe for him to fly back to Rome because he really wanted to go home as soon as he could. These boys don't get too much time at home and I thought it would be better for him to be where he felt most at ease, so rather than fly him back to England we arranged for him to be seen by a specialist in Rome who conducted a barrage of tests to make sure he was OK.'

Chapman is proud of the relationship he has developed with his two drivers. He says that he will never forget the occasion when he arrived at the circuit medical centre after Fisichella's crash. He recalled, 'Giancarlo was stretched out on the table with his blood pressure being taken and just about everything else being tested and he looked completely bewildered. When I walked in his eyes widened and lit up as if to say, "Well, I feel safe now." That's the sort of confidence and relationship you develop. It's not just a case of building up the muscles, it's just as important to create a trust. The connection you can make

mentally with a driver, and the help you can give him as a confidante and usually being the last person to attend him before he
goes onto the grid, is crucial to his confidence and his overall
well-being.

Chapman gets a great deal of job satisfaction from his role. He
says, 'It is fascinating to be that close to a top-class sportsman in
the last throes of his build-up. More and more people like me, in
the job I am in, are providing an important service in sending the
driver on to the grid not only at a peak of physical fitness but
reminding him and boosting his confidence that he is ready and
perfectly prepared in mind and body for the job in hand, no
matter how arduous or challenging. And from my own point of
view it doesn't half give you a kick and a whole load of satisfaction.'

GARY ANDERSON
Jordan Technical Director

There were not too many Formula One teams that suffered as many disastrous and disappointing setbacks as Jordan in 1998. The majestic domination of the championship by McLaren and Ferrari only served to put Jordan further in the shade.

If the gloomy bulletins issued from the headquarters opposite the main gates of Silverstone had been describing the condition of a hospital patient, close relations would have been busying themselves finding a burial plot. The death rattle was the frequent wheezing and clunking of a car with terminal problems. Owner Eddie Jordan was frequently left confused and staring bleakly at the post-mortems on the corpse in his garage.

Frustration first showed at the Spanish Grand Prix in Barcelona in May when Jordan's drivers disappointed: Damon Hill's engine broke and Ralf Schumacher finished eleventh. When asked about the race, Jordan said tersely, 'There is absolutely nothing I want to say about today's race. Let's forget it and move on to Monaco.'

But the misery mounted when the principality offered no reprieve as Hill finished eighth and Ralf Schumacher, who was consistently failing to get to grips with the need to be quick but restrained, retired with broken suspension. This time the team's owner described the race as 'a pretty sorry end to a very, very difficult weekend. Right from the beginning we were not able to overcome the problems we have. It is one of those weekends you need to forget. There are no excuses for our performance.'

He then went on to say: 'I know we need to do a lot of thinking and decide how to eradicate our problems. There will have to be some changes because we need to become more competitive as soon as we can, although I am aware there are no quick fixes. I think we will have to go through some pain before things get any better. I cannot fault the drivers, I have no question marks over them. It is very difficult to be upbeat in circumstances like this, especially when you put your life and soul into it. We all do, the whole team of 150-odd people. But I am the team leader and I must try to give some encouragement because everybody needs to be motivated again. I want to show people that their hard work will eventually pay off.'

Jordan was right when he said that it would take a while to turn things round. Further disappointment awaited at the Canadian Grand Prix, where both cars suffered mechanical difficulties and failed even to finish. Jordan said then: 'What I feel cannot be printed. We have to keep faith.' The pain was pretty evident. Jordan seemed to have lost his bounce; even the normally ready smile had a forced look about it.

It was strongly suspected that the team's major sponsors, Benson and Hedges, were not happy that the golden glow of their livery was beginning to look tarnished and that the win they wanted so much did not appear to be in prospect. But when Eddie later revealed the sponsor's reaction to the situation it turned out that the truth was somewhat different. He said: 'B and H came up trumps and helped rescue the situation which was pretty dire and not getting any better. They pumped even more money into the team, extended their contract with us, and we were able to afford to get down to doing the work needed to turn things around.'

The bulk of the workload fell to the Technical Director, Gary Anderson, a big and broad-shouldered down-to-earth fellow with an intimidating presence that smacks of authority and single-mindedness.

He started his working life tinkering with tractors as a twenty-year-old in Sevenoaks, Kent, close to the Brands Hatch race circuit where a friend helped out at the racing school, but he has come a long way since he first learned how to use a spanner. Anderson is happy to explain how he arrived in Formula One. He says, 'I left my home town, Coleraine in Londonderry, Northern Irealand, on 4 February 1972. The date still sticks in my mind. Don't ask me why. But I fancied a bit of change from Coleraine and London or thereabouts seemed a good idea. I'd never even been on an aeroplane and I had only been out of Ireland once, to go to the Isle of Man for the TT races. Then the guy who gave me a job messing about with tractors took me along to Brands Hatch and suddenly I was awakened to the magic of motor racing. Inside two months I was in Formula One, working for Bernie Ecclestone at Brabham.

'I had written to his team asking for a job. Over and above my enthusiasm and the knowledge I had picked up working on the cars at the Brands racing school, I didn't have much going for me – no university education, no degree, no impressive engineering qualification. So I guess I wasn't too surprised when Brabham's manager Colin Seeley, an old motorbike racer, wrote back and said there was nothing doing. But I was surprised a day later when I got a letter from Bernie saying there was. Like he has done with so many other people he took a chance on me and took me on.

'I was just one of a lot of people who lived off his back. A lot of them couldn't have made a living in the real world and certainly they would have struggled without Bernie's help. Some very big names in the sport these days should be grateful for his generosity. They'd have been nowhere without it. And they should all remember that he can make or break people in Formula One. He owned and ran Brabham and now he owns Formula One.'

Anderson believes that internal politics and too many consultants with too much to say contributed to Jordan's difficulties and put pit lane's most upbeat and cheeriest team into reverse. 'I would love to be able to spend more time sitting down and doing my doodles, getting things right for the car without any interference,' he says. 'But that's a dream scenario and nothing resembling the real situation. Unfortunately, in this business nowadays you get involved with too many other influences – the politicians around the place. I just get weary of having to fight them because it is all so stupid and it just gets harder all the time.

'Drawing designs, working on the car, doing your best for the team and the company is how it should be without complications. But it seems to me that I have been wasting my brain power, my mental capacity to solve problems, by being caught up in politics. I guess it's the same in any company. But in Formula One there is so much money involved, so many people with their own views on what is right and what is wrong and just about everything else because they want to get a percentage. It just frustrates all your efforts when you are beating your brains out trying to do your best without somebody sticking their nose in. I am a doer, a thinker, and if people put me in a corner against my will and better judgement I get irritated; if they leave me alone to get on with it and work it out I am good at that. That's when I am happiest and at my most productive. Give me a couple of hours on my own without being badgered and I will usually come up with the solutions. It's the so-called advisers who can screw it all up for you. But there is never a time when you get exactly what you want or need when those more interested in playing politics are around.

'It seems it doesn't make any difference that you have designed every Jordan car, dreamt about it, worked on it, perfected it and, like the 7-UP car, turned out a real beauty. Suddenly things aren't right for one reason or another and suddenly everybody is telling you how it should be done, suddenly they all know better. My reaction is to get out of the way and shut myself off because I know that when push comes to shove and I am left to fathom it out I will do it. And it will be right. It pisses me off because everybody's got an idea that is most likely to be a load of bollocks, but they've got to have their say.'

Anderson's frustration with the early-season performance

of Jordan was crystal clear as he went on to say: 'Nothing gives me a greater rush of adrenalin than being told we have got a major problem and that it must be fixed urgently. That's when you have really got to come into your own, use your initiative and experience and know-how and fix the bloody thing. I'm not the sort of guy to be shoved around by anybody. I know what I am doing without anybody telling me. This is my job, my life, my hobby, my sport and my love. And I just cannot get on with people who are not good at their job and yet try to tell me how to do mine. It is something else that irritates me, that and incompetence. And consultants. They are only consultants because they can't get a proper job in the first place or hold one down when they've got one.'

There were rumours that Anderson was going to leave Jordan because he was so frustrated by the team's performance and the abundance of advisers. He admits that he was tempted to leave Jordan once before. 'I nearly left a couple of years ago because of similar problems and it would have broken my heart because I love working for Eddie Jordan,' he says. 'We have come through a lot of bad times together and stuck with each other. We are pals as well as him being the guy who pays my wages. And that depth of friendship and trust is a rare commodity in Formula One.'

Trust is something that Anderson values highly and he believes that his relationship with Eddie Jordan is a huge advantage in the cut-throat world of motor racing. He sees parallels in their relationship and the one between Bernie Ecclestone and his supporters. He says: 'When he (Ecclestone) has given his blessing to whatever it is you want to do because he thinks it is a worthwhile project, beneficial to his beloved Formula One and don't forget he is no charity glad-handing everybody you know you have earned his friendship. And unless you cross him it stays that way. It is the same with Eddie Jordan. We have had our ups and downs through the years but he is a genuine guy and the differences have soon been forgotten and I honestly don't know too many people who dislike him.'

Anderson then went on to describe how increasing responsibilities had had an effect on Jordan, saying: 'He may not smile as often as he used to do and maybe he is not as happy-go-lucky as he was, but that is the way the whole business has changed for him as it has got bigger. Everybody wants a piece of him or a chunk of his time because we have moved away from being that cosy team with the family atmosphere. We are on the world stage now in a big way with sponsors piling in with millions of dollars and all naturally wanting a good return for their money. Part of the deal is Eddie's time: his being nice and his attendance at functions and meetings all over the globe. He can't do everything but he doesn't half try. It is hard under that weight of pressure to be grinning all the time.

'The team has grown beyond all the dreams we had when it fired up its first engine and ran its first race. We started it all together and we will finish it together.'

Ulsterman Anderson has masterminded every Jordan, including the aesthetically beautiful and effective 7-UP sponsored car, from the team's entry into Formula One in 1991. But in 1998 he was faced with the mammoth task of turning things round in the middle of the season. His one advantage was that he now had the money to invest in a programme of recovery. This was fortunate because the first thing that needed improving was the car's aerodynamics and that involved costly wind tunnel tests. Anderson's painstaking processes of improvement and elimination long into the night turned a flop into a competitive car. More than eighty alterations were made to the car and with Mugen-Honda, the engine suppliers, piling resources and specialists into the recovery project, the car became a winner for the first time at the Belgium Grand Prix in 1998. Not only did Hill win the race but he was followed across the line by his teammate Ralf Schumacher.

Eddie Jordan's delight manifested itself in an ecstatic jig down the pit lane in Belgium. Jordan also received a champagne drenching on the podium and £1,000 from the bookmakers for backing Hill to win at 10–1. Seventy people on a subsidized £20-a-head two-day trip from the Jordan factory, decked out in T-shirts, flags and banners in the team's colours, rejoiced with him. 'Suddenly it is summer,' commented Jordan. 'It seems to have been a long cold winter. But we have turned it all round. We have come back virtually from the dead which is where we were at Monaco. This is one of the success stories of the season.

'It would not have been possible without the resources from our sponsors. In years gone by Jordan would not have had the financial backing, but now, thanks to our improved marketing strategy and the growth of our profile, we have the budgets to keep moving forward. I never dreamed we would be able to close the gap like we have. And now we can travel to each race knowing we can be competitive, and think which teams we can out-perform instead of worrying about keeping our heads above water. Racing has become fun again.'

As Jordan celebrated, back in England Anderson was already working on the car for the 1999 season.

DENYS ROHAN
Chief Executive, Silverstone

T ucked away inside a triangle of country lanes, the sleepy hamlet of Dadford becomes totally isolated one Sunday every summer when Silverstone stages the British Grand Prix. From before dawn until well after nightfall more than 40,000 cars and coaches clog the road arteries that carry the 120,000 spectators to and from the circuit.

Paradoxically, for the thirty or so families who for the rest of the year enjoy the peace and rural tranquillity characteristic of backwater England, the noisy and relentless grand prix invasion renders them the most secure community in the country.

Their safety is one of the many responsibilities of Denys Rohan, Silverstone's Chief Executive.

Dadford may be only a cluster of houses that barely shows as a speck on the ordnance survey map, but to Rohan it represents a victim of his show every year. He explains: 'We have to try and compromise as best we can and we don't want to paralyse the entire community. A place like Dadford gets cut off and nobody can get in or out from about 6 a.m. on Sunday until late into the day, so I organize police and fire-engine cover, a doctor and stand-by medical helicopters just for the village, to make sure they are properly covered. If anybody got hurt or say, a baby was being born, the patient would be in hospital quicker from the village than on any other day of the year. We pay for it all and I consider it an essential part of our duty to the people who are inconvenienced by the upheaval the grand prix carries with it.'

Rohan's office is in a low-rise block fifty metres from the busy main gate at Silverstone, a far remove from his surroundings when he worked for Gerald Ronson, the disgraced tycoon fined a record £5 million and jailed for his part in the Guinness share-rigging scandal in 1986. Ronson owned the Heron Suzuki-GB operation and Rohan, a trained accountant, went to work for him as Finance Director in 1975. He was quickly promoted to Commercial Director, then on to Managing Director and, finally, Managing Director of Lancia.

'I spent a long time with Gerald and for part of the time I was responsible for the Suzuki motorcycle grand prix team,' says Rohan, explaining how he arrived at his present job. 'Since then I have had a consuming passion for racing; but when Heron, the group Gerald owned, changed its character I decided it was no longer really for me. I left without knowing really what I was going to do contemplating semi-retirement, I guess, but with no specific agenda.

'I was back home in South London, sitting by my swimming pool and wondering what the bloody hell I was going to do with the rest of my life. I had worked hard over the years at Heron, my children were grown up, and I was musing on taking it easy. Then right out of the blue I got a telephone call from a firm of head hunters in London asking me if I would be interested in taking over as Chief Executive of Silverstone. I couldn't believe it. It was the opportunity of a lifetime. I had no idea, still haven't to this day, who had put me forward for what must be one of the greatest jobs in motorsport.

'The challenge of working at Silverstone, the definitive grand prix circuit, was just too tempting to even think about resisting and I moved in at the end of 1993. In truth, I suppose I spent about two minutes thinking about whether I should accept the job. I used up a three-week touring holiday to the south of Spain just sitting in the car thinking about the things I could do, what improvements and ideas I could bring in. So by the time the trip was over and I got to the interview for the job I had a fairly reasonable notion about what I would do with the place.'

Rohan's reputation as a smooth operator and as a man who knows the accountancy business backwards, allied to his awareness of the burgeoning commercial possibilities of motorsport, was already widely appreciated. His work, for instance, with the Suzuki-GB motorcycle grand prix team and his handling of Barry Sheene and, later, Mike Hailwood during his remarkable comeback (he won the 1978 Isle of Man TT at the age of forty), had stamped him as a shrewd operator with a keen eye for a promotional opportunity.

At the time Rohan took the job at Silverstone he was worried that he might try to run before he could walk. 'My initial concern, I remember, was that I might try to do too much too quickly because there were so many opportunities for improvement, advancement and initiation and it was a question of getting things prioritized and patiently working at them and knocking them off the list one by one,' he says. 'Now we have 150 people working here full-time. Another 350 work part-time, related to various events. And on grand prix day there are around another 5,000 people working on site. It's a big crew of people with the extras coming among security guards, kitchen and serving staff.'

Rohan accepts that there are advantages and disadvantages to running a course that's financial success depends on one day of the year. On the one hand they have plenty of time to prepare for the grand prix but on the other, they are short of income streams for the rest of the year. However, there are little-known assets behind the scene. 'The British Grand Prix is pivotal to the success of Silverstone, the way it is structured and the way it is shaped at the moment,' says Rohan. 'The circuit is own by the BRDC (the British Racing Drivers Club), which is a completely altruistic organization and it is there only to foster British motorsport. It does not pay dividends, it does not even pay its directors. Any money we make is re-invested back into the circuit. If you make £100 you've got £100 to do something constructive, either with the sport or with the circuit, a magnificent environment for everybody whether you are a driver, a worker here or a visitor for the racing.'

Work on the race begins a lot earlier than you might think. 'The British Grand Prix rules your life for the six months leading up to it and the six months after it has gone,' explains Rohan. 'We have to start work on it about six months before it actually happens and right after the 1998 Grand Prix we are already working on the 1999 event. That's because when you print the 1998 programmes you have got to be telling the spectators what is going to be available next year what the seating structures will be like, how many seats there are going to be, laying plans for advance bookings and giving as much information as you can about marquees and parking and everything you can think of that the spectator wants to know so that he can make his plans with the minimum of fuss.

'So, in fact, you are talking fifteen months in advance, working off longer and longer lead times to make the job easier for the staff and trying to smooth the way for the spectator who is, after all, our lifeblood. And we must do our level best to make them happy and content; that is something we never stop working at.

'In summer 1998 we started moving on our Millennium Grand Prix and we needed to. The reason is that the Olympics are on in Sydney. You might think that shouldn't affect us. You'd be wrong because it has caused a world shortage of seats and marquees and we have had to place our bookings from our usual supplier in England for the year 2000. If we had left it any later all the seats would have been down in Australia. That's how critical the forward planning has to be.'

Under Rohan's guidance a lot of money has been invested in Silverstone. 'Since 1994 we have spent £12 million on the circuit,' he says. 'That's a massive outlay in just four years, but we have to keep the place right up to scratch. You cannot skimp when you have a circuit like ours, with its reputation worldwide and its appeal to race organizations. And you can't spend that sort of money on the basis of a one-off grand prix, it would too expensive. So there has to be continuity because the seriousness and the degree of the investment and the returns you get from it mean you have to take a five-year view. You have to ensure that you do have a five-year contract all sewn up in order to recover the financial commitment; to do it as a one-off when you have to spend such vast amounts of money to create and maintain the infrastructure, renders it impossible to make money.

'At Silverstone for the British Grand Prix there are three parties involved: Bernie Ecclestone who, simply, provides the show, Paddy McNally and his company who are involved in the sponsorship, the promotions and the advertising relating to the event, and ourselves. And, primarily, we are involved in terms of income and so on with the tickets that are sold on the gate. There are other bits and pieces to help the cashflow, but mainly our income stems from ticket revenues. We have an agreeably pleasant working relationship with both Bernie and Paddy where, while ultimately the contract rules, there is a huge amount of common sense applied to situations by all parties. If, strictly within the letter of the contract, it stipulates we can't do "X" but we can do "Y", we can talk it over with Bernie and Paddy. If it makes sense for everybody to change things around on a "yes" without it being written down, we do it. The bottom line is to make sure that the grand prix is a success and is as enjoyable and entertaining as we can make it with the minimum amount of fuss and red tape.'

Rohan is in the process of sewing up a deal with Ecclestone to safeguard the future of Silverstone. 'We already have an agreement in principle with Bernie for the following five years,' he says. 'That will be firmed up into a detailed contract inside the next eighteen months. But it is not a very convoluted negotiation – it is quite reasonably straightforward.

'There are outside influences to consider, like the Concorde Agreement where we have to comply with what the teams require and the implications of their demands. But generally and traditionally it is straightforward, certainly not a complicated issue. As far as I am concerned, right now, the deal for 2001 to 2006 has been done and it probably won't get revisited in any great degree or detail.'

Rohan enjoys the way in which Ecclestone works. 'The amazing thing about dealing with Bernie is the speed and simplicity with which he operates,' he says. 'Forget the notion that a contract will be hundreds of pages ours is ten maybe. And not closely typed. It is, he believes, important to get the fundamental principles right. I can't remember us ever having a sticking point. He understands the need to work quickly and decisively. There's no point in him driving us skint, he's a member of the Club!

'Bernie doesn't get involved with too much of the ordinary detail on what we do year in year out, but he does have a higher level of input. He likes to steer us in the right direction in terms of giving a better service to this group or that or to the teams and can we make it easier for them to get in and out because they have to struggle through the appalling traffic.

'He, of course, has this fantastic travelling circus of Formula One and his responsibilities as well as making money are to make life as easy as he can for the teams, the drivers, the media and the whole entourage that goes all over the world sixteen times a season.'

When the circus comes to town at Silverstone the ticket takings alone are huge. Rohan says, 'There are lots of figures, all of them on the highly classified list, but it is easy for anybody to work out that the gate receipts are just over £10 million.'

The day of the Silverstone Grand Prix presents tremendous

logistical problems, as Rohan explains. 'Race day, Sunday, is limited to 90,000 people but with the private, VIP guest and hospitality areas like the Paddock Club, which holds 3,500, the BRDC with its 1,500 visitors, the eighty suites that hold twenty-five people, the various little pockets of people and the staff there are just over 100,000. They have all got to be moved in and out, watered and fed and kept safe insofar as is possible with anything to do with the motorsport.'

Rohan also has to set up a once-a-year airport that is said to be the busiest in the world for just one day. 'We have a take-off or landing every nine seconds,' he says, 'from eight o'clock in the morning until eight o'clock at night. We do have a full-time heli-port at Silverstone, anyway, and we work with a company which specializes in air traffic control. But just for the grand prix we boost it and we have a major air traffic control set-up which is staffed by professional controllers brought in from airports and heliports all over the country. They handle what is a major and day-long air traffic situation.

'We take landing fees of around £17 a head and it is big busi-ness, but not major revenue for us. We don't make all that much out of it by the time we've set up the heliport terminals, put out the tables and chairs, organized the toilets, arranged the security guards and marked out the field and paid the airfield licence and the air traffic controllers. We don't take the entire amount people get charged for flying into here; we take the landing charges from the operators who are shuttling in and out of the place all day.

Silverstone is also the scene of a spectacular air show by the Royal Air Force, usually two hours before the 2 p.m. race start.

Nine Hawk jets of the Red Arrows display team perform their aerobatics over the sell-out crowd at a cost of £12,000.

'We hire them for £8,000 plus £4,000 insurance,' Rohan reveals, 'and that's one big bargain isn't it? I book them year on year and I reckon it is worth every penny. It's all part of the atmosphere: the speed, the noise, the whole spectacle of a weekend devoted to daredevil men performing all the deeds we ourselves would love to be able to do. It's sheer escapism and it's an essential part of our show. Not only that, it is our responsibility to give great value for money and whatever we can do to make the weekend memorable we feel is essential.'

A big headache for Rohan and his team is the army of campers who populate the fields around the track, some of them owned by Silverstone. 'A quarter of a million people and their cars and motorbikes and caravans descend on the area and some 28,000 of them camp out,' he says. 'They need water, for instance, and the village can't handle it, so we carry tanks of 100,000 gallons of drinking water and we pump it all over an 800-acre site.'

A by-pass has been proposed for Silverstone and Rohan hopes it gets permission as, he thinks it would offset the traffic problems caused by having 40,000 cars descend on the site. 'It would help Silverstone considerably but the discussions have been going on for twenty years and they are always "going to be decided shortly",' he says. 'It would ease our traffic flow problems along the main road that runs to the north of our site. It is horrendous, extremely busy and dangerous and one of the few stretches of road that I can think of that is carrying such a massive weight of traffic where people's drives go straight from

41

their houses into the road. From the Silverstone village point of view it is essential; from our own viewpoint it could reduce our traffic exiting times by about forty-five minutes. It is not going to revolutionize the problem, but it will turn a terrible, terrible race-day traffic jam into a terrible race-day traffic jam. When you are moving 30,000-plus cars, and you get one going through the exit gate every four seconds, it takes six-and-a-quarter hours to clear the site.'

At the moment Rohan is using ingenious methods to alleviate the density of the traffic on race-day. 'We love to take the pressure off the home-going rush by attracting people to stay on and enjoy barbecue parties with lots of people staying overnight and camping,' he explains. 'And, of course, we usually have our own little pop concert in the paddock after the races when we let the fans into an area they normally can't enter. It's a fantastic night organized by Eddie Jordan. He's a keen drummer and he has all these pals in showbiz who just want to get up on stage and jam it up and all for free. You gets the likes of Chris de Burgh, George Harrison, Chris Rea, all world megastars playing alongside Damon Hill, who is a dab hand on the guitar. Drivers like Eddie Irvine and Johnny Herbert, and anybody else who wants to join in, sing and dance with the band. It would be impossible to plan. It's an ad lib situation, but it attracts the fans and it is as rewarding for them to see their heroes, usually regarded as the untouchables, relaxing as it is for the drivers to be able to do it.'

The Jordan show, staged on a makeshift platform on a huge truck, has been the noisy finale to every Silverstone Grand Prix but one for a decade. In 1998 it was off because Jordan and most of the pop stars who would have played piled into a private jet and flew to Paris for football's World Cup Final.

Jordan, who has played in rehearsals with Chris Rea and busked on radio at the Australian Grand Prix with George Harrison, says, 'It's great when all these people come together – music and motor racing – to have a high old time. Silverstone opens the paddock that is normally as tightly closed and guarded as a prison camp and the public can come in, have a few beers and enjoy a concert that would probably cost them £25 if it were done just as a show and not as a bit of a giggle.

'In a practical sense it is far better to be standing around with your pals or your family, maybe having a beer or two and watching some of the world's great rock stars doing their stuff for nothing, than being stuck in a nose-to-tail crawl home when you had a nose-to-tail crawl to the track in the first place.'

Despite the efforts of men like Rohan to popularize the sport Jordan feels that there are still improvements to be made on the public relations side. 'Formula One has become isolationist so far as the public is concerned and I think that the sponsors, who in the final analysis are paying the drivers' wages, could do a lot more to insist that their stars go out and meet the crowds face to face,' he says. 'I would be more than delighted to establish the requisite facilities to make sure that the drivers were safe and were not going to get swamped or mobbed. The driver either wants to do it or he does not and he is the only person who seems to have the say and he seems only to want to do it when, in rare cases, a sponsor points out that he is the one signing the cheques, so do it.

'The rationale would be to have a mandatory autograph and

photo-opportunity session at every grand prix. It makes good sense and it would bring the drivers back to the public. That has to be good PR for everybody in the sport.

'In Formula One I think that all the British drivers would be up for it. If they weren't maybe a little prodding in the wallet would encourage them to do it. Or have them do it for charity. It certainly presents lots of opportunities to create goodwill. Of course, we all know their time is precious but the real value in Formula One is that people should want to come out and watch it, feel part of it and be committed to the live show. Driver contact is a vital ingredient in that. It creates a grand prix lifestyle and if people don't want to watch the race either on television or in the flesh then we don't have a business any more. I firmly believe it is the characters and their identification and contact with the punters who make the sport buzz.'

It is interesting to see how Silverstone has developed over the years since it staged the first post-war grand prix in Britain in 1948. That race, organized by the Royal Automobile Club (RAC) in just two months, was a logistical nightmare in the days of post-war austerity and shortage. More than 100,000 people, mostly carried in charabancs because petrol was rationed and private motorists were few, saw a pair of Maseratis dominate the race with thirty-eight-year-old Italian Luigi Villoresi, a prisoner of war only three years earlier, winning after driving at an average of 72 mph. He had started from the back of the grid because he turned up too late for qualifying. His prize money was £500 and Pathe Pictorial ran newsreels of the great event in cinemas throughout the country a week later.

At that time Silverstone had only two small grandstands,

rope barriers separated the spectators from the cars, and officials worked in tents alongside pits that were improvised from scaffolding framework.

Half a century later the scene at Silverstone has changed beyond all recognition and Rohan and his predecessors must take credit for that. It now costs £15 million to run the British Grand Prix for a four-day crowd of 250,000, either standing on the banking or sitting in the ten grandstands with their total capacity of 53,000. The television audience is reckoned by Rohan to be 350 million in 130 countries. There are thirty-nine custom-built brick garages in the pit lane with piped water and electricity and the circuit has its own TV service with giant screens around the 800-acre estate. More than 400 journalists from all over the world arrive to cover an event where 5,000 or so track staff are employed to work an eighteen-hour day.

There is a magic about Silverstone that is irresistible. It doesn't have the same showbusiness allure that makes Monaco such a glittering and exciting place but it generates a vitality of its own. The four-day festival is organized perfectly – it is a masterpiece of speed and spectator indulgence.

WILLI WEBER

Michael Schumacher's Manager

W hen Willi Weber completed the formalities of an extended four-year contract with Ferrari for Michael Schumacher in 1998, it became the longest and most financially rewarding in the history of Formula One and certainly among the biggest in world sport.

The bottom line on the deal is a yearly pay cheque of around £25 million which, with add-ons, bonuses and personal sponsorship arrangements (all planned and put in place by Weber), boosts the German genius's bank balance by at least double that figure. What's more, this does not even take into account Schumacher's worldwide commercial and merchandising operation which, in 1998, was reported to be turning over more than £70 million a year. Another part of the deal is that Schumacher will play an ambassadorial role for the company long after his retirement as the longest-serving driver in the history of the Maranello team.

Ferrari's appreciation of Schumacher's towering skill matches their admiration of Weber's ability to squeeze the maximum out of any deal without causing ill feeling.

After the contract had been signed Weber heard Gianni Agnelli, whose family controls FIAT, say: 'Michael is the finest driver in the world, especially in difficult conditions. He has the talent of a genius. And as Enzo Ferrari would have said, his great characteristic is that he has three, four, five or six horsepower in his feet alone.'

As Schumacher's manager Weber had considered several other bids for the German's services. He had held extensive talks with McLaren-Mercedes before he and Michael got together for final discussions on the historic Ferrari plan at Schumacher's Geneva lakeside home in mid-summer 1998.

Weber's role in the nurturing of Schumacher into a world star has been a mix of sheer professionalism and friendship. A decade of correct moves, clever negotiating, smooth organizational standards and absolute trust between Schumacher and Weber has been the blueprint for others to try to match.

Weber revels in the recognition he enjoys because of his high-profile association with the man universally regarded as the greatest driver of his generation. The two first met in 1988 when Weber owned the most successful Formula Three team in Europe. Weber explains, 'I was always on the look out for young drivers to carry on my success. I saw Michael Schumacher racing in Formula Fords and I kept an eye on him for more than a year because I wanted to see if his driving was consistent. Then in autumn that year he had a race at Salzburg in Austria where my team was competing. I watched his event and he started from seventh place on the grid, but after the first lap he was leading by twenty seconds. I wasn't so much impressed that he was the front runner or that he won the race it was the way he handled the car. His feel for it, the balance and his car control was just fantastic. You could see he was a natural-born racer, very intelligent in the way he ran his race, but with this marvellous ability that stamped him as extra special.

'His skill made my thinking very clear; this was a great driver of the future and I needed him in my car. I talked to him and offered him a test drive in Formula Three. He was completely surprised but happy, too, that I was offering him a fine chance in a good car in a successful team.

'When he ran in my car for the first time he was every bit as fantastic as he had been when I had watched him and he had been streets ahead in Formula Fords. I made up my mind there and then to have him in my line-up and I offered him a contract without money to join us. It was like Christmas, Easter and his birthday had all come on one day for him. And, later, for me too. But it was the beginning of an amazing relationship. Ten years on it is stronger than ever.'

It soon became plain to Weber that his discovery was developing into a major asset that needed careful and considerate nurturing in a motorsport world hungry for such a promotable clean-cut figure. In fact, Weber was so convinced of Schumacher's appeal that he decided to curtail his other business interests. 'I had three hotels and thirty-five restaurants and it was a good business which I enjoyed and it had been my life. But when we came into Formula One, it was evident that I could not afford to divide my attention and Michael became my priority interest. I sold everything I had built up. Sure, it was a risk and it was a strange situation, but it was clear to me that I must take care of him and his business interests. We were travelling a lot and I realized that this was to be my life and that I could turn my hobby into my business because I had a good understanding of how to handle all the potential pitfalls and all the possibilities that were taking shape. Michael agreed and in 1993 I sold everything and committed myself 100 per cent to him.

'We now have twenty-five people working for us and I look after all the merchandising, which is huge business all over the world. I arrive at the track early, long before qualifying and racing, to talk to partners and sponsors and keep them happy while Michael is getting on with what he does best. It is the same programme at every race ... sixteen GPs, in Europe, Australia, Japan and Canada. And I am there by Tuesday to talk to people, to make sure we are maintaining contacts with business associates.'

Due to his relationship with Michael, Weber is often asked for help by other sports stars. But, he says, 'this is not working as a manager for them, it is just being a friend. I do it on that basis, not for the money or the business. I don't need their money.'

If the rumours are true he certainly doesn't need any extra cash. It is believed that Schumacher cuts Weber in for 20 per cent of his earnings and Schumacher was earning around £1 million a race in 1996 and 1997.

Weber is clearly proud of his relationship with the former world champion and more than happy to talk extensively about it. 'We have never had fall-outs or any difficulties and we do not argue,' he says. 'From the very beginning of our association it has always been beautiful. To go into Formula One like we did, when we were running together for success and success was running right behind us, it was like starting something which was perfect. And even if you work, as I did, sixteen hours a day, the feedback is so fantastic and Michael is so good to work with that the rewards are amazing. As hard as it has been and despite the problems and troubles we have faced from time to time I would not miss one day if I had to go through it all again.

'I am not his mentor, his teacher or his trainer. I want to be his picture, I suppose. He sees me. He dresses the way I dress, the way I believe is best for him to impress, with stylish suits and neat business-like shirts and ties and he says, "OK, that's OK, that is the way I need to be."

'When we were first together he would look to me for advice; what kind of watch he should wear; how he does this and that; and how to have a friendship based on advice and trust. I made my suggestions gently but firmly, in the way you do when you want to keep a relationship without upsetting somebody. I did it, not with my finger waving and saying "no" or "you must not do this because I say so" because any other way would have been wrong and clumsy. This is not the way we work together.

'We discuss things, whatever comes up, and we decide between us what action we should take. I can't remember there ever being a shouting match … never in ten years. I give my feelings and my opinion based on my age, my knowledge of life and long experience in business and he gives his view from a different perspective, right from his stomach as a gut reaction, because of his youth and, compared with mine, his lack of experience. We put it all together and, usually, come up with a good result.

'Michael is now one of the most famous faces on the planet. He cannot go anywhere without being recognized and that is due to his unbelievable talent as the greatest racing driver of all time. If I have helped to promote the personality and shape the image by making sure he said and did all the right things and looked correct then I am happy; but it pleases me more that I have been able to help him with his contracts and his finances and be a good friend, confidante and, sometimes, counsellor at the same time.

'I never imagined in the beginning that he would ever be as famous as he is now. Sure, I had a great feeling that he was something special, something a cut above the rest. And when he was driving my car and then won the Formula Three championship my instincts were awakening.

'But when he drove for the first time in Formula One in the Belgian Grand Prix in Spa in the Jordan in 1991, I knew then that all the feedback I'd had from him was soon going to show itself on a much bigger stage in a way that few of us would ever forget. The satisfaction I have from being part of it is the reason why, I suppose, I am one of the happiest men in Formula One.'

The cynical might suggest Weber's unbridled joy stems from the huge slice he takes from Schumacher's earnings, but their relationship is clearly based on mutual respect. Schumacher's intense concentration and attention when his manager is making his opinions felt and Weber's blatantly obvious indulgence and unashamed pride whenever he is in Michael's presence or just talking about him makes this clear. Their partnership is envied the length and breadth of the pit lane where petty squabbles and in-fighting frequently divide and destroy relationships, often because the manager wants more attention than his client.

Formula One is riddled with dissolved partnerships where agents, managers and mentors have overstepped the mark and overstayed their welcome around the pits by attempting to interfere in the running of a team. One so-called advisor to a fast-rising star driver not only bungled his client's chances of a championship drive with excessive demands, but made himself vastly unpopular by hanging around in the hurly-burly of the garage during a race and occupying valuable space. Another, widely regarded as a nuisance in the pits and asked by the team chief to stand outside during a race, seems to spend as much time as he can squeezing himself into the frame of any photographs taken of his driver.

Weber, by contrast, is on hand if needed by Schumacher but, unless he is invited, he is rarely in the same TV shot or photograph as the man he regards as a superstar. 'The background is where I prefer to be,' he says. 'That is where I do most of my work for Michael. I don't need to be in front of the cameras or saying things for him. He is quite capable of speaking well for himself. He does not need me to be there. But if he wanted me to then I would.'

When Weber began to fashion Schumacher's future beyond Benetton after his second successive title in 1995 he knew that Shell and Marlboro, Ferrari's new backers, had money to burn and were prepared to lure the champion to the legendary Italian team. Every other major team, made aware by Weber of Schumacher's readiness to quit Benetton, agreed to a cartel ceiling figure of £10 million, believing that he would simply opt for the car with the best chance of another title. They were then staggered to find themselves seriously short in their bidding.

The decision to join Ferrari had two attractions for Weber: the massive amount of money he could get for Schumacher, more than £1 million a race with bonuses, and the romance of the marriage of the famous marque to the greatest talent available. Schumacher would have to reach deep into his rich reserves of skill to get the best from a developing car that in its better, more co-operative moods was little more than wayward. Ferrari certainly wasn't a championship challenger until 1997 and 1998 when Schumacher revitalized the team.

Weber explains, 'When I pushed Michael very hard towards Ferrari it was the start of a dream for me. It was not so much so for him because he was too young to understand the full impact and romance of the Ferrari name. I knew all about their legend, their history, their image. But for him it was just a red car. A race car, sure, but just that. He couldn't fully understand the background to the name but he soon learned and now he knows very well the importance of the legend. It came very quickly to him after he started driving for Ferrari.

'If he hadn't joined Ferrari from Benetton he might have gone to Williams or McLaren. But when we spoke about it, even though Williams then was the car to beat, Michael was strictly against the idea because he reckoned it would have been too easy for him to sit in a car like theirs and win sixteen races out of seventeen. And that, he said at the time, was not the sort of easy way to the title he wanted, any driver could do that. He wanted a bigger challenge than that, he didn't want an easy ride and I agreed. I knew Michael as a man who loves a fight and he was looking not so much for a good car as one that could be developed into a fantastic platform for his talent. He ruled that the car must not be a front runner so that he could show his performance like he did with Benetton.

'The most satisfying and appreciated achievement for a

driver is when, like he did, you take a chance and join a team whose car is not strong enough to win the championship but you turn it into a winner with your confidence and an ability that compensates and makes up for the car's deficiencies. You turn it all round and change the disadvantages and when you win the title, as he did with Benetton in 1994 and 1995, it is the greatest feeling you can have.

'Ferrari fitted the requirements of the challenge he preferred to have to the Williams or McLaren money in the bank. The car was certainly not a clear world championship prospect when he joined. But he changed all that and he will further the legend.'

And what about the lifestyle of a legendary manager? Weber smiles under the grey beard, assumes an exaggeratedly theatrical German accent and opens the forefinger and thumb on his right hand about two inches saying: 'Ja . . . I have a leedle, leedle houze on the Riviera and a leedle, leedle aeroplane and I have no time at all to use them.'

Thanks to Michael on all counts, no doubt.

MURRAY WALKER
TV Commentator

The man who likes to be known as the voice of motorsport was reminiscing about racing over lunch at his local pub when he was interrupted. 'And what, might I enquire, do you do for a living young man?' asked the genteel dowager in the twin-set and three layers of pearls at the adjoining table as Murray Walker's eyes widened in disbelief across his poached salmon.

His super-charged, high-decibel commentary style, described by television presenter Clive James as sounding as if his trousers were on fire, and his moon face and trademark spectacles may have made instantly recognizable in Australia, New Zealand, Bombay, Japan and right across the Far East, but in the village pub barely a mile from his Hampshire countryside home, Murray's fame had evaporated.

'Well, madam, I talk about grand prix motor car racing,' was his patient answer to the elegant, but rather ancient lady who happened to be seeking an after-dinner speaker for a charity function she was organizing and had been told by the landlord, who felt no job description was necessary, that Murray might be just the man for her. She replied, 'Oh dear me, such a smelly and noisy business. That will never do. Thank you all the same. But could I ask, without being personal, why on earth do you do it?'

She then added, rather sniffily, 'especially at your age.' 'It's all I know,' Murray replied resignedly.

Murray's straightforward response summed up his lifelong commitment and complete surrender to motorsport ... and it said much about his self-effacing attitude, even after fifty years behind the microphone, first for radio, and now for ITV after establishing himself as a folklore figure at the BBC. He even had his troublesome and extremely painful hips replaced so that he could carry on commentating and he says, 'In this job, contrary to popular misconceptions, the work doesn't revolve only around the commentary box and the microphone. And it is essential to get up and down the paddock to find all the gossip and all the latest news. You have to be able to talk to drivers and team people so that you can give the fullest information for all those millions of viewers who are hanging on every word.

'My hips were playing me up so badly because of all the wear and tear over the years and it was getting really difficult for me to walk without being in agony. I couldn't keep up with my requirement to be among the teams in the paddock and I was worried that the job would suffer so I had both my hip joints replaced.'

That's the Walker way. If there is a sacrifice to be made for the sport that is the enduring love of his life then he is prepared to make it. And that included not having a family. 'Truth to tell,' he says, 'motor racing is my passion, my life. And, quite honestly, I don't regret not having children. Because I don't have any kids there is nobody to follow the family tradition of broadcasting started by my father Graham when he used to cover motorbike races.

'I like to think I would have been a good father, but I am not desperately upset that we don't have any children. It just did not happen and I have never aspired to being a dad, though I've got nothing against kids. I certainly did not feel that my life was incomplete without an offspring.'

Damon Hill, who has known Murray since he was a child, calls him Dad. 'He is such a lovely father-figure, we all have such tremendous affection for him,' says Hill. Murray responds, 'I really am extremely fond of Damon and have been since he was just a toddler. And I am old enough to be his father. That is why it was one of my happiest, proudest and most emotional moments of my long, long career when I could talk him home to the Formula One championship in Japan in 1996. That was really memorable and I will carry it with me to my grave.

'Moments like that when you have a personal interest make this job so magical. I just love being involved. I enjoy all the travel and the fantastic atmosphere at the races wherever in the world they are (and I cannot think of anything else I would rather do … except, perhaps, be a top level driver. But what better, if you can't be a racer, than to be paid to go and watch the finest Formula One events and commentate and talk about the sport to your heart's content to hundreds of millions of people all over the world?'

While he admits to being the oldest broadcast commentator around he qualifies that by adding that he is also 'probably the most enthusiastic'.

Murray has two sessions a week in a gymnasium to keep himself in trim. He proved his fitness when he comfortably passed the rigorous medical necessary before he could ride in the revolutionary two-seater 200 mph promotional McLaren MP4-98T. The car was driven with considerable bravura for eight wearying laps, five in the wet, three in the dry, by co-commentator Martin Brundle, the former F1 ace, before the rain-sodden British Grand Prix at Silverstone in 1998. 'That I have to confess was the most thrilling experience of my life,' he says 'A modern Formula One car is like a bucking bronco when it's driven like Martin was driving it – hard – and snapping from corner to corner and apex to apex. I was very tired, but extremely exhilarated, at the end. It may play havoc with your neck muscles – and I was wearing a special brace – but it is such a stimulating experience that it can put the fear of God into you. It doesn't half boost the adrenalin flow.'

Home for Murray is a sprawling bungalow which lies in splendidly idyllic isolation at the end of a rutted lane on the fringes of the New Forest. The shelves in his study are a mass of motorsport memorabilia: books, trophies, programmes, souvenirs, photographs, model cars and motorbikes – and a picture of him riding tandem at 200 mph with Brundle. Murray says of that race, 'That was the ultimate sensation. I wasn't too scared – just a bit nervous and keyed up. I felt as safe as houses with Martin and when he asked me over the radio link if I could manage five laps on the trot I said I'd do it if it killed me.

'I am unashamedly a racing nut. Everything about the sport, the noise, the colour, the characters, the atmosphere, excites me. And to have had that sort of close-up of what it feels like to be in a Formula One car, or the closest thing to one, was just sensational because, quite frankly, I am a frustrated race driver I would love to have been Murray Walker, Formula One world champion or Murray Walker, 500cc Motorcyle Race world champion.'

He did achieve a modicum of success on two wheels. He says, 'I was pretty good at club trials events – and I did manage to win a gold medal at the International Six-Day Trial in 1949. But that was the year when a lot of riders won gold medals.' It was also the year he started as a broadcaster.

Murray's unique commentary style, pitched somewhere between hysteria and amnesia, endears him to most fans who regard his slip-ups with affection – but the same errors, nowadays gently and almost unobtrusively corrected on air by Brundle, can infuriate enthusiasts who endure them with diminishing patience and frequently write letters of complaint to the specialist magazines.

Colleges up and down Britain have Murray Walker cult fan clubs and wear T-shirts emblazoned with his fauxs pas, many of which have passed into broadcast folklore. Murray can recount most of them himself. In his typical self-effacing manner Murray, also known as Flurry Squawker and Muddy Talker, has a rare ability to laugh at himself. He enjoys his rather bizarre motormouth celebrity but he gently protests that he feels some of his bloomers have been embellished in the re-telling.

A post-race interview with his friend and television pizza commercial co-star Damon Hill went as follows. Murray: 'Damon, tell me, when did you first become aware you had a puncture?' Hill: 'When the tyre went down, Murray.'

Others, frozen for ever in the film archives at the BBC and ITV and screen printed for posterity onto T-shirts, go like this: 'Now, now excuse me while I interrupt myself,' 'You can't see the digital clock because there isn't one', 'And now the boot is on the other Schumacher', 'Either that car is stationary or it's on the move', 'Prost can see Mansell in his earphones', 'Damon Hill is leading ... behind him are the second and third men', 'The atmosphere is so tense you could cut it with a cricket stump', 'Just under ten seconds lead for Nigel Mansell ... call it 9.5 seconds in round figures', 'And Nelson Piquet must be furious with himself inside his helmet', 'He is watching us from hospital with his injured knee', 'I imagine that conditions today are totally unimaginable', 'We are looking at the man who won in 1983, in 1985 and in 1986 ... so this could be his hat-trick', 'Do my eyes deceive me, or is Senna's car sounding rough?', 'With the race half gone there is half the race to go', 'He has obviously gone in for a wheel change – and I say obviously because I can't see him', 'I can't imagine what kind of problem Senna has ... I imagine it must be some kind of grip problem', 'You can see that the gap between Mansell and Piquet is rather more than just visible', 'Once again, Damon Hill is modest in defeat' and, most famously, 'Unless I am very much mistaken ... and I am very much mistaken' which has become a Murray motto.

His attitude to his mistakes is to say, 'I don't so much drop horrendous clangers or make mistakes, I make prophecies that go wrong straight away.' He adds, 'Sometimes, when I have said something in the heat of the moment which I know right away is wrong, I want to grab the wires and strangle them before the words can get down them. But (it is) too late and somebody in Workington or Wagga Wagga is left thinking what a silly old bugger I am. But I don't do it on purpose, I assure you. I can't help myself. I get so wound up and excited it just seems to come out.'

He was convinced he had lost his beloved commentary job when Bernie Ecclestone favoured ITV's offer of £70 million for a seven-year deal to cover grand prix racing over the cash-starved BBC's paltry £7 million. He says, 'When I heard about the switch I was totally shattered. I seriously believed it was all over for me and I thought about jacking it in then and there. I thought it might be an appropriate time for me to announce that I was quitting. I felt that my reputation as a commentator was as high as it was ever going to be. And, suddenly it seemed as if the time was right for me to go. Damon Hill, my good friend, had won the world title and that, I have to confess, was a truly emotional personal experience for me. So, all things considered, I told myself it might be an appropriate moment for me to retire.

'After all, I was seventy-three and I reasoned that I was not getting any younger and that at my age things start falling off and failing, physically and mentally. I had done every televised Grand Prix for the Beeb since 1978 and I had worked for them before that on radio from 1949.'

It was a bleak and uncertain time for Murray as different names were bandied about almost every week to join the ITV commentary team. There was clearly nobody at ITV suited to the job and so candidates from Eurosport and Sky TV were considered. The wait for Murray was agonizing because, by now, his name was being mooted on the basis of his instant identification with Formula One and he was becoming increasingly hopeful that he could stave off dreaded retirement. Pessimism persistently outweighed optimisim in his mind, however, and the curiosity of concerned people in the Formula One paddock about his uncertain future only served to further unnerve him. All he could do was put on a brave face and respond to all the queries, 'Don't know, old boy, don't know what's happening.' ITV, meanwhile, were anxious to harvest a younger audience and flirted with the notion of hiring somebody trendier than the old gentleman in the trainers and polo shirt.

They found the ideal compromise. They decided to pair Murray with Martin Brundle, a quick-witted and down-to-earth personality with humour and racing expertise. Brundle proved to be a natural commentator and the perfect foil for his veteran colleague. But it took a lot of persuasion by ITV to get Brundle to agree to a regular job with them. He still harboured hopes of a Formula One drive so it was written into his contract that if he did get an offer from a team he was to be released. As a millionaire, tied in with his brother in a successful car sales business in Kings Lynn, Brundle didn't need ITV nearly as much as they needed him and was therefore in a strong position to dictate terms.

ITV's choice of Brundle was an inspired move. He very quickly established himself as a star with his neat, if cheeky and irreverent, line in confident and informative interviews on the grid just before the start of a race and in trailer-features. His style had been just what Ecclestone, with his sense of showbiz, had wanted and what the BBC had always failed to deliver. The Murray and Martin Show was born.

Murray's wait, despite his misgivings, had been worthwhile and he was relieved he hadn't announced his retirement. 'When ITV called me and asked me to head their commentary team I could hardly believe my luck. To say I was thrilled is a massive understatement. And I got a few quid more! To be in a second phase of a career like mine at my age has to be just about the most satisfying feeling of all. I suppose if I had retired I would have spent all my own money roaming the world going to grands prix. I certainly could not have stayed away for long.

'OK, I am seventy-four. I am a human being – a strong one maybe. But I am going to start to wear out. Eventually I guess I won't be able to keep up either mentally or physically – but I will know before anybody else. I will be the first one to recognize that I am going ga-ga. Then I will stop. I won't try to continue like some silly old fool who doesn't recognize his sell-by date has passed. Anyway, what's age? A number or two. It is what's in the head, the attitude and the enthusiasm that counts. And I have no worries on that score. That's the great thing about Formula One ... it is full of competitive people who live for a challenge. It doesn't matter who you are in racing or what job you do, whether you are a driver, a team boss or a commentator, the competition is fierce. You have to be on your toes around so many clever people who can be ruthless in their aims. They are all out to take your job and destroy you and you have to have the talent and the determination to resist and climb above them – behind the wheel or the microphone. It doesn't matter.'

The contrast between Murray's present and former commentary box colleagues Martin Brundle and James Hunt, both grand prix drivers of note and summarisers of reflex and great self-belief when they took up the microphone, couldn't be more distinct. Brundle, says Murray, is a broadcaster par excellence with a wonderful insight to the sport and a knack of getting his point across without causing offence. 'Martin is so full of wickedly dry humour,' he says. 'He is wonderfully entertaining and he has so much know-how and such a wonderful way of delivering his views, concisely and clearly with great economy, that he is going to become just as big a favourite on ITV as James was with me on BBC. He keeps me in line.'

Martin, surprised to discover that Murray commentates standing up in front of a monitor and swaying with the action, told me, 'I found myself caught up in the scene, doing the same thing, one arm around Murray's shoulders, swaying to and fro. And, suddenly I thought, anybody looking on from the outside the commentary booth must have thought we looked like a pair of windscreen wipers.'

The Hunt connection, however, did not get off to the same smooth start and Murray reveals, 'There was some chemistry between us that worked very well – but in the early days James was an idle bugger. He would arrive about five minutes before the race began, having worried the life out of us that he wasn't going to turn up at all, then at the end, as soon as the chequered flag had fallen, he would instantly disappear from the box as if he had a synchronized spring up his backside. I reckoned him then to be an arrogant, self-opinionated Hooray Henry who drank too much and took drugs. And he had this rather cavalier habit of absenting himself from the box and we'd find him on the steps puffing away at some rather strange substances. I reckoned none of it was my business just so long as he was doing the job properly, which he did. And I have no complaints about that.'

Hunt, the 1976 Formula One champion, was a notoriously

high-liver. When he died of a heart attack at his Wimbledon home in 1993 he was almost penniless. When he was commentating it was clear that he didn't particularly admire or even like drivers such as Nigel Mansell, Riccardo Patrese and Nelson Piquet. It was easy to get him fired up on air at the mere mention of their names. 'It was one way to get a torrent of invective from him about what he regarded as the uselessness of Piquet and Patrese and how miffed he was that Mansell, the all-British hero, had let the side down so badly by deserting Formula One to go racing IndyCars in America. I always knew I could get a reaction out of him by saying something complimentary about them,' says Murray.

There were many moments of drama within the commentary box during the fourteen years that he and Hunt were co-commentators. Murray recalls how Hunt almost had the plug pulled on him when in a typically rash and outspoken attack live on air he called Jean-Pierre Jarier, the rather less than successful Ligier driver, a 'French wanker'. Murray recalled that Hunt added, 'Always has been. Always will be.'

Murray says that he and Hunt had to work hard to form a successful broadcasting combination. 'We changed our attitudes to accommodate each other,' he says, 'and he became much more mature and more fun to work with. So much so that we became really good friends.'

Even so the normally placid Walker could be stirred to rage by Hunt's supercilious manner. 'One year at Silverstone I was so bloody furious with him I actually had my fist above his head ready to hit him,' says Murray. 'We almost came to blows – he had pulled the microphone out of my hand. The producer intervened and stopped me hitting him. I am not easily aroused but I was bloody furious with James that day. I am quite sure he regarded me as a pompous old fart who talked too much.'

Murray will forever be remembered for his distinctive style. Peter O'Sullevan, the long-serving BBC horse race commentator who was regarded as the best in the world in his field said of him, 'He has the great gift of having a voice and a delivery that makes him instantly recognizable. You can be in the far reaches of your house, well away from the TV set, and you know, aside from the roar of the engines, when Formula One is on because of the unique sound of Murray's commentary. There will never be another quite like him. And we forgive him his occasional blips because he really is extra-special.'

Even after fifty years of high-pressure work behind the microphone Murray is generally regarded by the drivers with a great deal of affection and esteem. The relationship with his Formula One fellow travellers is something which Murray holds close to his heart, as anyone who has seen presentations being made to him, when he is frequently reduced to tears, knows.

CHRIS DE BURGH
Rock Star and Formula One fan

Having flown in from a Save the Children Fund concert, Chris de Burgh picked his way through the celebrity-packed paddock formed along the busy quayside at the Monaco Grand Prix. He side-stepped the throng around Sylvester Stallone who had travelled up the coast from the Cannes film festival to do some research for a Formula One movie he is planning and nodded at Manchester United's super-star footballer Ryan Giggs, but adroitly avoided getting caught up in the rush of cameramen and onlookers bustling around film star Liz Hurley. She was standing alongside her actor boyfriend Hugh Grant but gazing with unashamed admiration and long-ing at Eddie Irvine in his scarlet Ferrari overalls. Chris, a firm friend of Irvine's but not anxious to deflect the Hurley focus, walked on, neatly by-passing the cliques of George Harrison and Phil Collins on their way to lunch at Eddie Jordan's celebrity stopover. He was happy to be anonymous in the mêlée. De Burgh had his permanent VIP pass, issued personally by Formula One supremo Bernie Ecclestone, around his neck, and in the pockets of his trademark black leather blouson were invi-tations to drop by for drinks or a meal at McLaren, Jordan and Williams where music lover Jacques Villeneuve, one of his biggest fans, wanted to have a chat.

De Burgh is a petrol head. 'And I am not ashamed to admit it,' says the pop idol, one of the late Princess Diana's favourite singers, whose albums have sold millions and whose songs form the soundtrack to many people's lives. But he confesses that the music he likes to hear is the sound trumpeted deafeningly through the exhaust pipes of an 800 bhp 210 mph Formula One car.

'I wouldn't miss any grand prix anywhere in the world if there is the remotest chance I can get to it. I just love the atmosphere and the excitement it all generates. It has an extra special buzz and I get caught up with it so much and so deeply it gives me little shivers. I guess there isn't a bigger fan than I am.'

Soon after Mika Hakkinen had won his first Monaco Grand Prix, Mercedes team director Norbert Haug was blasting tunes of glory from the motorhome sound system and the Monte Carlo streets were alive with celebrating F1 fans. But de Burgh's busy schedule meant that he was already flying home.

He sprawled in the comfortable leather of his eight-seater Citation jet as it nosed skywards from Nice Airport. The sight of drivers behind the wheels of missiles of cars that accelerate from standstill to 120 mph and back to a dead stop in barely six seconds was still a vivid picture in his mind's eye. Like any football fan returning home, but at 30,000-feet and in sheer luxury, Chris excitedly replayed the action and enthused over the relative merits of the men he admires most.

'It has got to be the most exciting sport there is,' he said. 'The performance of those cars just blows your mind and the guys who do the business behind the wheel at places like Monaco, where you've got to have inch-perfect precision between those barriers because your life depends on it, are just supermen to me.

'I just couldn't do that job and they have every bit of my admiration for their courage, their talent and their complete dedication and the intelligent and icily cool way most of them go about it even when everything around them seems to be going crazy. I don't know how they manage to keep so calm and so much in control and focused when there are so many different things to think about and so many problems to deal with aside from the driving.'

Although de Burgh is clearly fascinated by speed he wouldn't necessarily recommend it. When he spoke about his first introduction to real velocity he recalled, 'Nigel Mansell, the year he won the championship, gave me the scariest white-knuckle ride I have ever had in my life. He drove me around the Spa-Francorchamps circuit in Belgium. And I will never forget it, it was absolutely terrifying for me. I finished up all of a tremble and he was only driving a small family saloon. At its quickest it was about half as fast as he would go in the race.

'When we had done a lap, and I was still shaking and amazed that we'd survived in one piece, he asked me if I'd enjoyed it. And I hadn't got the guts to admit that he had scared me witless so I answered "yes". That was a big mistake because he thought he'd continue the treat and do it all over again. And it still frightened the bloody life out of me. But when you get that close to watching a world-class grand prix driver at work it does fill you with awe and wonder at their skill. Then you remember when you are out there with them, believing you are right on the edge, they are only using up a fraction of their ability one-handed at that and telling you what is going on and where you are on the track, when you are sitting there wishing they would look where they are going and stop talking.'

De Burgh is clearly in awe of motor racing. 'It was a tremendous privilege for me when Bernie Ecclestone gave me a pass to go to every grand prix in the world,' he says. 'And I get to as many as I can. I love standing on the edge of the grid at the start of a race. It is the most sensational feeling and buzz when those great big sleek monsters of cars are unleashed and the engine roar when they blast off bites into your very soul. Honestly, it makes the hair on the back of my neck stand up. And you know there are twenty-odd adrenalized guys, all equally committed, determined and brave and in no mood to give way, blitzing in a crazy charge in what I can only describe as an ear-splitting rush of sound at 180 miles an hour to a corner that they can only get through two abreast at the most. And none of them is prepared to be the first to give way or back off. Now that is awesome. That is having raw courage.

'You can feel the sensation and atmosphere and thrill of it all right to your insides and it boils you up. That, for me, is just about the biggest kick you can get and unless you have experienced it close up and first hand you never get the same sense of reality on television you can't imagine the affect it has on you. And I've played in front of some pretty big and wild audiences and felt the emotion and the appreciation coming at me. So I do know a bit about that buzz.'

For de Burgh, one of the great pleasures of Formula One is the opportunity he has to mix with the people in the sport. 'The characters are unforgettable,' he comments. 'And I just love Eddie Jordan's approach. He always makes me promise to bring my guitar to the races so I can play afterwards. Silverstone, after the British Grand Prix, is usually a great night. Eddie organizes a big party and they let the punters into the paddock to join in. I play a bit, so does Chris Rea and Nick Mason, the Pink Floyd drummer, and anybody else who can do a bit gets up on stage. Eddie Jordan is pretty nifty on the drums and Damon Hill is a more than useful guitarist. He loves to give it some stick and you get the likes of Johnny Herbert, David Coulthard and Eddie Irvine singing a song or two.'

Having mixed with the stars of Formula One de Burgh has formed close friendships with some of the drivers, although sometimes with mixed success. He says, 'I have been trying to teach Eddie Irvine to the play the guitar but it's a useless exercise. I am wasting my time. I have been up to his house in Dublin a few times and tried to teach him a chord or two so he can get by but he hasn't got a musical note in his head. And the only lesson he has learned is that he is better off sticking to his driving. A guitarist he will never be.'

Chris, as unassuming and as modest as he is clever in his song-writing, can't believe the respect he is shown by the stars of the grid. 'I am frankly amazed just how many people in Formula One recognize me and know and enjoy my music,' he says. 'It is very flattering. It was staggering to me when Michael Schumacher got out of his car to shake my hand on the grid as if I was some big shot. Truth is, I have spent more time in this music business of mine falling from a great height into a bucket of muck than I care to recall. But I guess that is all part of the process like it is for these guys and just like them you have to fight for what you want out of life. You have to be able to take the knocks and climb back on your feet. Just look at Eddie Jordan and Damon Hill winning in Belgium when they had been at rock bottom only a few races before. That's the magic of feeling you always want to be a winner.'

De Burgh sees analogies between the music business and motor racing. 'In my own sphere I have learned to appreciate absolute excellence and that is why I admire top sportsmen like finely tuned racing drivers who have to be courageous all alone, to carry through their aims and convert their talent into achievements and championships,' he says. 'And when you see the likes of Michael Schumacher, a complete genius, riding on the very edge in the far reaches of technology in the tipping rain and looking as if he is power boating, you have got to stand back, take stock and realize that what you are witnessing is something magically special, and appreciate the enormity of what he is doing under complete control. That makes Formula One unforgettable for me.'

De Burgh does have a burning ambition to make his name in Formula One, but not on the track. 'I've got a secret yearning,' he says, 'and, no, it's not to race or be driven round the circuit. I'd love to make my own mark in Monte Carlo by being invited to sing again at the Grand Prix gala.'

De Burgh's dream weekend would involve motor racing at Monaco. He says, 'I would go off and play golf with my old pal Ian Woosnam, watch qualifying and then the race, which would be fabulous as it always is, and end up having a marvellous dinner with Schumacher and Irvine and Eddie Jordan and the

rest of my heroes and enjoy all the good crack that would go
with a night like that, then sing and play for them. That could be
a riot.'

CRAIG POLLOCK

**Managing Director,
British American Racing**

Craig Pollock, the guiding force behind Formula One's newest team, British American Racing (BAR), has the clean-cut and healthy appearance of an athlete who has just stepped off the ski slopes despite the fact that he has been working a twelve-hour day in a stuffy office in London's West End.

Pollock is a fiercely motivated and shrewd individual who has, in a few short years, rocketed from his job as a physical training teacher to become someone who helps shape the destiny of Formula One with the support of multinational companies' sponsorship money.

Born in Falkirk in 1956, Pollock graduated from Jorden Hill College, Glasgow University, with a degree in sport and biology. He took up a job as a ski instructor and physical education teacher in his homeland before moving to Switzerland to work as Director of Sport at an exclusive boarding school. One of his pupils, and the daredevil star of the ski slopes that were a backdrop to the school, was Jacques Villeneuve. Pollock, fifteen years older, developed a kinship with the speed-mad youngster and an admiration for his spirit. Although they went their separate ways when Villeneuve left school and Pollock became a sports clothing salesman in Switzerland they kept in touch, little realizing that their paths would cross again in a professional capacity. Pollock was invited to join the Honda Motor Corporation on a consultancy basis and when he took up the position he was involved with work concerning the Formula One television rights. 'The only experience I'd had of motor racing,' he says, 'was doing a bit of marshalling at Ingleston, the race track not far from my home in Scotland. So it was a whole new world to me. But it seemed exciting and I was hungry to know more about it particularly as Jacques, the son of a very famous father in racing, had grown up under my guidance and was heading towards racing.'

As Pollock's business ambitions and interest in motor racing developed Villeneuve was gaining a reputation as a precociously skilful teenager who, it seemed, had inherited his father's feel for the dangerous game but he could not get a deal with a team worthy of his signature.

The pair met up again in Japan where Pollock was selling TV rights and Villeneuve, along with Michael Schumacher, Mika Hakkinen, Mika Salo and Eddie Irvine, was trying to launch a Formula One career. 'It seemed like it was destined to be,' said Pollock, 'but when I bumped into Jacques in Japan it seemed like he was lost. He wasn't quite sure how to set about organizing himself outside the car. He was OK when he was behind the wheel, but he was useless outside his overalls. So, just because he was a friend, I took him under my wing. It was like being back with him at school in Switzerland.

'He asked me no, he bloody well badgered me to be his manager. He was desperate. And I refused twice. Then he asked me a third time he just would not get off my back and I agreed

Schumacher's sensational F1 debut at Spa with Jordan, replacing the jailed Bertrand Gachot. (Above)

A young Michael Schumacher hones his motoring skills (Left)

With Benetton at Spa, the first Grand Prix victory of his career, 1992. (Below)

Schumacher crashes into the barriers at the Belgian Grand Prix, 1996. (Right)

First place in the Ferrari at the Argentinian Grand Prix, 1998. (Far right)

At speed on his way to a stunning technical victory at the Monaco Grand Prix, 1995, the year he became the youngest ever double World Champion at 26. (Below)

Willi Weber. (Right)

The team at work at the Hungarian Grand Prix, 1998. (Left)

The result of hard team work - one driver climbs the walls with joy. (Below)

Super fan Chris de Burgh jams with Damon Hill. (Above)

Silverstone from the air. (Opposite)

Murray Walker at the racetrack, Silverstone, 1997. (Top opposite)

Jacques Villeneuve and Craig Pollock, an unlikely couple. (Below)

Max Mosley discusses the new Concorde Agreement, May 1998. (Right)

Bernie Ecclestone asks Ron Dennis if McLaren can get any higher up the grid. (Below)

to look into the idea after he had worn me down. I guess it all started from there. And we have never looked back. I have to say now that it was one of the best moves I ever made. Jacques is so easy to deal with and get along with.'

Events moved pretty quickly after the pair reached an agreement. Villeneuve had been struggling for three years with inadequate machinery in Formula Three in Italy so Pollock decided to place him on the fiercely competitive Japanese junior class scene where he would either survive and thrive or come up short against the challenge of the upcoming Formula Three and Formula 3000 drivers. But the wins suddenly started to happen as Villeneuve's confidence, boosted by his partnership with Pollock, soared.

Pollock was delighted at Villeneuve's breakthrough. He recalls, 'All of a sudden Jacques looked like the driver we all felt he could be. Given proper time in the car and decent machinery to work with he soon started to learn how to drive as a racing driver with a great future. And there were some useful guys around, all with a point to prove and, they hoped, a chance to get into Formula One if they could show up well in Japan.'

But Pollock and Villeneuve did not go straight to Formula One. Instead, they went to IndyCar racing in the United States where Villeneuve drove a made-in-Britain Reynard car and was backed by huge financial support from BAT, under the Player's Limited Green colours. In 1995, the team won the IndyCar title in only their second year of partnership.

After all they have been through together Pollock feels a strong bond with Villeneuve. He says: 'There have been three highlights in my association with Jacques: when he won the

Indy 500, when he became the IndyCar champion and when he won the Formula One championship in 1997. I have to confess that each time, and I am a pretty cool sort of guy usually very much in control of my emotions, I was overcome with pride. I must have come close to bursting with joy. I guess I am as close to him as I am to my own son not that Jacques needs a father figure. What he needs is to have the best and most genuine of friends around him, not people who suck up to him or just want to be in his company because of who he is but honest people who tell him the truth.'

Although they are clearly kindred spirits the contrast between the appearance of the two men could not be greater. Pollock dresses in the sharp suits appropriate to a powerful man who spends a great deal of time in the formality of boardrooms while Villeneuve cuts an anarchic and eccentric figure. His downbeat grunge gear, his jeans gashed at the knee, his unbuttoned scruffy tartan shirt over a T-shirt flopping outside his waistband, trainers and his either blond- or lilac-dyed and thinning hair combine to make him look more like an underground busker than a Formula One millionaire.

The sponsor of Pollock's team is British American Tobacco (BAT), the cigarette manufacturing group which had sponsored them in their IndyCar days. BAT decided to divert some of the profits from the 700 billion cigarettes they sell each year into Formula One after listening to Pollock's suggestion that he become an equity partner for their investment. BAT was an appropriate company to approach not only because of their links from IndyCar racing but also because it has a tradition of motorsport involvement dating back to the 1980s when it backed Nigel

Mansell, Ayrton Senna and Elio de Angelis in the striking black and gold John Player Special Lotuses.

In company with Reynard Engineering, his old IndyCar partner, and BAT, Pollock paid Ken Tyrrell, an admittedly reluctant seller, £12 million for his team. The decision to buy one of the longest-established teams in Formula One was a clever shortcut to gaining a foothold in the sport before the name change planned for 1999 when Tyrrell will become known as British American Racing. It also gave them certain benefits, including monies from the teams' Concorde Agreement (a confidential document covering the funding and organisation of Formula One, including details of prize money and its distribution), splits of television fees and help with air transport costs for the expensive trips to Japan, Australia, Canada, Brazil and Argentina, and automatic membership of the FIA's Technical Commission.

BAT has committed £250 million in a five-year deal to Pollock and the company has retained partnership equity in the team instead of acting only as sponsors in the traditional marketing sense. Compare that with Jordan's turnover of £35 million a year where some 60 per cent of the sponsorship income is generated by Benson and Hedges and you can see that the team means business. With such strong financial backing Pollock was able to put in competitive bids for the best drivers. Naturally, he was soon in the bidding for Villeneuve. It is a reflection of the varied and fluid structure of Formula One, and the management of drivers, that Pollock continued to be Villeneuve's manager. At the time Pollock commented: 'The way things are going at Williams, the way they are not performing, is doing me a great big favour. Frank (Williams) wants to re-negotiate and we will compete. To my way of thinking it's a case of may the best man win and we still have a lot to prove. But it can't be a satisfactory situation for Jacques trying to defend his title in a car that it isn't doing the job for him. It's a shame because he is such a fine driver. I would love to have him in my team, but he must make up his own mind. This is where favours and affiliations don't come into it. He would have to join me on the basis of wanting to be in the team because he thought it could be a winner not because of any friendship, any dues imagined or otherwise, or feeling of loyalty to me even though I have always been concerned to do my best for him.'

Villeneuve did decide to abandon Williams and join BAR. His new salary was rumoured to be £10 million a year, making the contract the second richest in F1 after Schumacher's Ferrari deal, and around £4 million more than Frank Williams had paid him. When Pollock had secured Villeneuve's services he discussed his relationship with the French-Canadian, saying: 'Jacques owes me nothing. My reputation as a businessman and manager in motor racing is because of Jacques Villeneuve. I have shaped my life and built my business around him. And he has developed his career around my business. We have progressed forwards together and have helped each other out and have been crucial to the other's career decisions. So he does not owe me a thing and I don't owe him, either. We're quits. And when he came to the team he did it as a career move, not under the illusion that I was pulling any favours because I wanted a top-class driver, a proven winner. And I have to say I did not approach him or anybody else. But I'll tell you a secret, I had so many guys, big-name drivers, approaching me for a drive I almost lost count –

ten at least. Some of their bosses would certainly be surprised if I revealed who they were.'

But Pollock's ambitions for his team extended beyond signing the 1997 champion. He wanted the two best drivers for his team and hoped to pair Villeneuve with Michael Schumacher. However, the German, the hottest property in Formula One, opted to stay with Ferrari when they offered him £20 million a year, with bonuses and the guarantee of an on-going ambassador's job with FIAT after retirement.

Pollock explained his attempt to sign the German ace by saying: 'I reasoned why shouldn't I go for Michael Schumacher? There's nothing to be lost by asking. Our goal is to be winning in the shortest possible time and our expectation was that the car, the chassis, the engine and the back-up were all going to be excellent. All it needed was a top driver. Ask every team boss in pit lane who is the best, and they will all answer Michael Schumacher, with Jacques second. Well, I couldn't get Michael, but I got the next best in Jacques. It wasn't realistic to expect to have them both but, again, there was no harm and nothing lost in trying. There was a hell of a lot to be gained if it had come off … and you have to be seen to be on the gold standard.'

Even so, the fact that Pollock was able to sign Villeneuve was a major triumph and a clear sign to Formula One that he and the newest team on the grid meant business.

New ground was being broken on all fronts. And this time, unlike his IndyCar arrangement where he had worked for a small percentage of Villeneuve's earnings but unwisely held no equity in the team, Pollock covered himself by taking a slice of the financial action. 'I learned from my errors in IndyCars in the

States,' he says. 'There I was so busy looking after Jacques' interests making sure he was OK finding a good team manager in Barry Green, and working so hard. I ploughed a lot of money into the team and into him but I wasn't in charge and I didn't get anything back except my cut from whatever money I organized for him. I realized I had given it all away for what really was a small percentage of a salary.

'It took me a year to realize that what I should have done was retain an equity in the team. I was very foolish. I made a serious mistake, missed out on a lot of money and my big chance in IndyCars had gone. It was total ignorance on my part. I was too focused on making sure that Jacques was going to be in the best position possible to win the championship very early on in his IndyCar career.'

Pollock's decision to move from IndyCars to Formula One was a relatively easy one to make. He explains, 'I didn't consider running my own IndyCar team, even though it was an area of racing with which I was very familiar, because I had already set Jacques up with sponsorship and it isn't easy to get major backing again. To do it all over could have been harder than the first time. There is a bit of luck involved and you have to know when to ride it and how to recognize it and feel it when it comes your way; I reckoned I'd gone as far as I could. So I just thought, OK, let's change direction.

'Formula One, I thought, looked like an even bigger challenge. It interested me and it was certainly big business. I made up my mind that if I ever did go to Formula One and run my own team, and I started to think seriously about that around 1994, I wouldn't do it the same way as I had done the IndyCar deal. And this time I wanted to make sure I was the boss. I wanted to be in charge.'

When Pollock got the go-ahead from BAT he started to put a strong team together. His first selection was Julian Jakobi, as Corporate Director, an accountant and graduate from Oxford University, who had worked for the International Management Group (IMG), as head of their Monaco office. He was a specialist in management who had supervised the business affairs of tennis and golf stars, as well as those of Jackie Stewart, Alain Prost, Michael Schumacher and Ayrton Senna, before becoming Senna's personal manager. As if that was not enough of a portfolio to impress BAT, Jakobi had also guided conductor Sir Georg Solti and designer Ralph Lauren.

Former racer Rick Gorne was appointed the BAR commercial director. Gorne had won in Reynard cars before taking jobs in sales and marketing and briefly becoming competitions director for the British Automobile Racing Club. Under his direction Reynard cars won two Queen's Awards for Export Achievement, in 1990 and 1996; Reynard remains the only motor racing company to win the award twice.

Malcolm Oastler is the chief designer. A graduate of the New South Wales University of Technology in Sydney, he is another one-time racing driver. He competed in Australia in Formula Ford in the mid-1980s, finishing second in the national championships in his rookie year. After he quit competition to work in Britain at Reynard, his chassis designs won five titles in five seasons and when the Reynard IndyCar concept became a reality in 1994 Oastler headed the design team. His 951 chassis won eight IndyCar races, including the Indianapolis 500.

Dr Adrian Reynard is the technical director of BAR and he proudly boasts that the company is 'the only car manufacturer in the world to have won the first race of every major single-seater championship we have contested.'

Dr Reynard, the company founder and Professor of Engineering and Applied Sciences at Cranfield University in England, felt that Formula One was the next logical step for a team that had conquered every other branch of single-seater racing. When Pollock stepped back into his life to offer the challenge of taking on the best in F1, with big money backing, he couldn't resist. In 1997 his cars had virtually wiped out the opposition in America, achieving eight of the top ten places in the championship, with thirteen victories and fifteen pole positions from just eighteen races. There was nowhere else for him to go except to new frontiers. And that meant Formula One.

The likelihood of a repeat in Formula One may be a lofty ambition but it hasn't stopped Pollock dreaming. He says, 'To win straightaway had to be our aim. Why not? Why not pitch for the top? After all, look at Adrian's record. It's wonderful. In 1994 Reynard entered a car for the IndyCar World Series and it won first time out from the front row of the grid. Just a year later they drove away with the drivers' and the constructors' championship as well as the Indy 500 and the rookie of the year prizes. And they did it all over again in 1996. In 1997 they dominated the PPG Cart series by winning the drivers', the constructors' and the rookie of the year titles.'

Pollock's Formula One dream began to turn into reality in 1995. 'Adrian, Rick Gorne and I were having breakfast on the patio at my place in Indianapolis,' he says. 'They told me they had lost just about everything trying to put together a Formula One team. They had even built a factory, which Benetton later took over, but had to sell it to save the company from going bankrupt. Their problem, they explained to me, was that they didn't have the funding necessary to launch such a bold venture and they were in dead trouble. I asked them, "What if you did have the money and everything else in place would you still go ahead?" And I said that it would be really something if the Reynard organization could maybe move into Formula One and take on those guys.

'Adrian, always the practical thinker, said that sure they could, but only if the right amount of funding was in place so that he could compete with everybody on a level playing field. There was no hiding his excitement at the notion he was clearly intrigued at the idea. And having detected that in him, it was up to me to try and put it all into place. The thought had been burning me up for a while and I had a few ideas to work on. I didn't tell them. I didn't make any promises but I set about working like hell to get the backing to make the whole thing work.'

Pollock then explained how he had gone about securing funding for the project, saying, 'When you are looking for such a high level of investment and funding there is no way you can do it by cold calling. You have to do it through relationships, trusts mutually developed, built up over years. I have been fortunate that since around 1985 I have been involved in sales, promotions and television rights and I have a huge network of powerful and influential friends and contacts in major businesses all over the world. Sometimes you can pull on the contacts to open doors that would be closed to other people on the same mission: trying to raise money. People get to know and trust you. But you still have to be bold and you can't afford to blink or shy off and be timid when you are asking somebody for £20 million. You have to look them straight in the eye, then justify. Luckily, I have every confidence in my capacity as a businessman and if something I have to offer is logical then I have no second thoughts about calling somebody up with my proposals. If I didn't have belief in my ideas then there is no way I would even dare make an approach to a company like British American Tobacco. In this particular case I maybe had the advantage because I knew the sponsors better than a lot of other people who were also trying to persuade them to fund their Formula One operation. And they knew me and trusted me.

'I discovered that other teams up and down the paddock Williams, Benetton, McLaren had tried to get the same level of funding from the same sponsor. What I had to do was guide BAT to a different approach from that of the other teams and offer them a completely fresh outlook in sponsorship. They wanted a positive identity with a new Formula One entity: clean, sharp, with a plan to create a completely different image in the build-up of a brand. They accepted it would be easier and more preferable to develop a brand with a new team rather than an established one. So I agreed that what we needed to do was create our plans and proposals with the needs of the sponsors and not the team uppermost, which takes nothing away from the priorities of racing or the money that will be its lifeblood. But the image of the car will be brand effective and it will be a team with a distinctive personality, not remote, not cut off from the public.

Pollock's plans for BAR are well defined. He says: 'Our idea is that we will be different from every other team in grand prix racing and in many ways. Paramount to our thinking is that we will promote an openness and encourage a strong desire to be close to our audience. We won't be a team that is the private preserve or the toy of a rich owner. Our fans will have a claim. Formula One has been quite a closed affair in the past. We want to be upfront, and while we will still have a fierce commitment to excel it doesn't mean we can't be accessible. We learned that in IndyCars. You can produce a winning team in a really tough series and still be accessible to the people and the fans around you.

'We will be doing things in a fresh and open way right from the start. All the partners in the foundation of the team are highly experienced in motorsport each one, really, capable of running their own team and we all know the value of public support.'

BAT has drawn up a seven-point plan for the team. As well as being an example of the typically enthusiastic American approach to demonstrating wholehearted eagerness for a project it also seeks to harmonize the ambitions of Pollock and the sponsor. It begins, 'As the Formula One team of the future, the philosophy of British American Racing is to create an open culture which, combined with the experience and expertise it is assembling, will help the new entity achieve its ambitious objectives.' It continues by stating BAR's guiding principles: '1. Responsibly compete at the highest level of motorsport. 2. Be synonymous with engineering and performance excellence. 3. Ensure that improvement is the only constant. 4. Put safety on equal terms with performance. 5. Manage the business in a way

97

that delivers fair value to all stakeholders. 6. Allow each team member the opportunity to achieve their full potential. 7. Be open, be accessible and have fun.'

At the opening of BAR's 135,000 square-foot purpose-built factory and headquarters at Brackley, a fifteen-minute drive from Silverstone, Pollock made specific reference to the plan, saying, 'Our new organization's mission is clear: to make a positive contribution to the Formula One paddock and to win races. In doing so, I would like to think we could also have some fun along the way.'

Bernie Ecclestone, always ready to improve on his show and keen to have resilience and quality from the front to the back of his grand prix grids, welcomed Pollock's new team and its bright and innovative ideas into the Formula One fold by saying, 'This is good news, and it can only be great for racing. British American Tobacco has been committed to the sport for years and it is wonderful to see them back. Who can ever forget the marvellous achievements of those eye-catching cars in the John Player Special teams? We remember them with great fondness. They were a prime force in Formula One. Who's to argue that it cannot happen again?'

But perhaps Pollock should stop to think about the situation at the Stewart team. With £250 million of Ford money to spend it is still struggling to make an impact in its second year of competition. Unsurprisingly, Jackie Stewart has a word of caution for Pollock's grand plans. 'BAR have a fantastically reliable and well-proven engine in the Mecachrome. They have built a new factory and it would seem that they have endless amounts of money,' he says. 'They are in with Adrian Reynard, who is a really good partner and I think they will do a good job. But whether they can challenge the top teams, I don't know. Even the most experienced teams take time to gel and I think they will have teething troubles.' But Pollock rejects any negative thoughts. He says, 'We are going to do our best to win first time out. If not, I am sure we will soon be a formidable challenge to the established order in Formula One.'

Pollock's determination to succeed is hardly surprising given the tremendous personal sacrifices he has made in order to form his team. 'I am willing to work night and day and that's just what I have been doing since this project first formed as an idea,' he says. 'But when you see it taking shape and the dreams begin to take real form you suddenly know that all the sacrifices and all the effort have been worthwhile. It was my promise to myself that there was only one way to go and that I would have only the very best for the team: the greatest drivers and I got Jacques performing for the best engineers with the finest equipment, the greatest chassis and the neatest, friendliest most upfront team in Formula One.'

Pollock surrendered family life as he went back and forth across the Atlantic to set up and fine-tune the deal with his friend from IndyCar days, Tom Moser, the head of global sponsorships at British American Tobacco. 'If you dedicate all your energies,' he says, 'as honestly as you can to whatever project that has taken your fancy, and if you are prepared to make supreme sacrifices, even in your family life, then you deserve to succeed. I went weeks, sometimes nearly two months, without seeing my wife, Barbara, and my twelve-year-old son Scott and that was really tough on us all. But, thank God, they understood that I had to give the team all the attention I could.'

The family lived in Switzerland while Pollock commuted between there, his apartment in Monaco and a flat near to his office in London's West End. 'I was getting to my desk at 5.30 a.m. and staying until late at night every night,' he says, 'and the phones were on the go non-stop. But, honestly, I was having an absolute blast, a great time full of excitement and buzz and promise, even if it was wearying and time consuming. I just revelled in facing all the problems, working at them with my assistant and resolving them. And there were plenty, I can assure you. One of them was sorting through 1,300 applications for just ten advertised jobs in the team.

'But I have grown up in the atmosphere of hard work. When I was first with Jacques in IndyCars I moved to live in America for about two years to be close to the action. And when I was setting up BAR I was on the move constantly and travelling abroad so much it was a real trial. But I couldn't bring myself to move my son from school yet again. It seemed we'd had an upheaval about every two years and that's not good for a boy trying to settle into his education. So my wife and I agreed that we'd do it this way and leave Scott to get on with his schooling without interruption. She would stay in Switzerland and I would be based in London and Monaco. But we have not had a holiday for twelve years, not since Scott was born. The closest I came to one was when we managed to get away to Florida for five days. I spent the whole time in our hotel bedroom making telephone calls.

'You just have to get on with the hard slog, do your best under the circumstances and not complain. I even had to have an operation on a bad knee in Canada because that's where a lot was happening for me and I couldn't afford the time to go nearer home to have it done. The minute you fall away or let things slide is a disaster. You have to fight it and be alert and ready to make sacrifices. That's life.'

The alliance between Pollock and Villeneuve is strengthened by their close friendship. Now they are set to be boss and employee but their bond is so strong that the burden of mutual responsibility is unlikely to affect the relationship. Pollock says that when Roland Ratzenberger and Ayrton Senna were killed at Imola in 1994 it made a huge difference to his feelings for Villeneuve. 'It changed my attitude to managing Jacques. Being killed in a crash is just dreadful but it is final. To survive with injuries that leave the driver paralysed and completely dependent on others for the rest of his life is almost as bad.' Pollock decided to take responsibility for Villeneuve and encouraged him to think deeply about the need to invest in enough funds to ensure that he can survive as independently as possible in the event of a bad accident.

It is this sort of action that makes it clear that Pollock and Villeneuve are far more than professional colleagues; they are a team of friends. The backing of BAT may be crucial to the success of Pollock's team but it is his empathy with Villeneuve that will surely give BAR an added advantage over their competitors.

MAX MOSLEY

President of FIA
(Federation International de l'Automobile)

An unprepossessing doorway, brightened only by the glint of a discreet, well polished brass name plate, gives way immediately to a short steep staircase, which, in turn, leads to the camped inner sanctum of the FIA's President's office in London.

The headquarters in Paris, close by the Hotel Crillon where some of the world's most distinguished and famous visitors temporarily reside, is a far grander and crustily ancient pile. With elaborate cast iron gates, trophy cabinets in the long mirrored hall, a veritable warren of offices and creaky cage lift it has an exclusive, formal and clubby atmosphere.

The power behind the FIA and the link between the Kensington office and the Paris HQ is Max Mosley, a trained lawyer, a politician at heart and a stickler for fair play, respect for authority and good behaviour, how ever rich and famous and talented a driver may be. Despite rumours to the contrary, Mosley is a firm friend of Bernie Ecclestone, the President of the Formula One Constructors' Association (FOCA), the Vice-President of FIA, the commercial rights holder and the power behind the huge global success of Formula One. Together they have forged a formidable partnership which tolerates no threat to its pursuit of commercial success for Formula One.

Mosley is a thoroughly fascinating figure: intelligent, aristocratic, in control of his emotions and as eloquent, clever and physically imposing as you would expect a well-bred, sharp-brained lawyer to be. He sacrificed a career at the Bar – selling his wig for £15 – to chase his dream of becoming a racing car driver. However, the dream came to an abrupt halt when he crashed his Lotus at 150 mph at the Nurburgring in the 1960s. A year earlier he had taken part in the tragic Formula Two race at Hockenheim when Jim Clark, the brilliant Scottish world champion, was killed in his Lotus 48 at the notoriously fast Ostkurv. The two events served to convince his wife that racing was far too dangerous and Mosley's driving days were over.

But the grand prix bug had bitten and he founded his own team, March. At the same time he became friends with Ecclestone, who had bought the Brabham team. Together they assumed the responsibility for negotiating for all the F1 teams, soon becoming two of the most prominently progressive and outspoken figures in the sport.

Now the President of FIA his role is to 'look after the day-to-day running of the federation and to deal with the myriad of problems that crop up every day of every week.' Mosley came to the job through his work as President of the Manufacturers' Commission, a position where he came into direct contact with FIA. He explained, 'I was the guy who represented the whole of the world's motoring industry on the World Motorsport Council and I also headed a group of committees as chairman of the competition departments for the manufacturers. After about three or four years it got more and more difficult to get hold of anybody and I could never get anything discussed or any decisions made. I got so fed up with it all I decided I wasn't going to go on, even though it was a well-paid position. But, in the end, I reasoned that there was no point in simply walking away from it all. Because there was an election coming up I thought I'd try and get myself elected as President of FIA and stand against the rather autocratic President of the time, Jean-Marie Balestre. He was a real hard man to take on and challenge and he ruled with a rod of iron.

'I thought I'd get one of the clubs around the world somewhere to put me up for election against him. I did a lot of canvassing, but there weren't too many ready and brave enough to take me on because they knew failure would be certain death for them. It is one thing to vote in a secret ballot and have no focus fall on you and quite another to put your head over the parapet and reveal you are supporting a complete outsider like me against a well-established and much-feared man like Balestre.

'In the end it was New Zealand who decided to back me. The reason New Zealand put me up was that they were very unhappy with the way the federation was being run. So, too, were a lot of other countries and once I had found one country to back me and face up to Balestre then it all started to come together. There were still great risks, though. Balestre was a powerful and wily old campaigner even though he had never been seriously challenged before. And I could have fallen flat on my face.

'It is normal, of course, even though I was getting good vibes from all of the countries I had talked to, that some people will always say they will give you their support because just in case you don't get in they don't want you to think they weren't ready to help. Mind you, there were a certain number of countries who came straight out and said, very nicely, we have known you for a very long time, we like and admire you and what you are doing, but we are not going to back you. In the end it turned out that most of them did.

'I suppose that my background as a former racer, a team owner and as a committee representative and my reputation with Bernie as an organizer in grands prix, had gone before me and I had been all over the world meeting people over the years. I didn't then know people in rallying, but they knew of me through my work on the Manufacturers' Commission and the World Council and one way or another I was a familiar character to a lot of key figures who enjoyed a sphere of influence and who could bring other countries in behind me.

'It is history now, but I beat Balestre and got elected. I think he found it difficult to believe it had happened but he behaved very well and accepted it as sporting defeat. I certainly could not criticize him because he was dignified about the whole upset even though he must have felt a lot of pain and disappointment. We remained the best of friends and he handed over FIA, so to speak, voluntarily and without demur.

'Afterwards we created the Senate and he became President of that and he has really worked hard with me. Except for one or two little hiccups and disagreements he has been impeccable.'

Mosley felt that he was well qualified to take on the challenge of FIA's presidency. 'For the position as President I felt you needed two aspects of knowledge: technical understanding and a basis of law,' he said. 'I had studied for a degree in physics at

Oxford, and even though it was a long time ago, it helps me enormously to understand the technology of cars and what makes them tick and, of course, my background in law as a practising barrister has served me equally well.'

He also felt that there were other areas of experience that made him suitable for the job. He had been a co-owner of a company building racing cars for about eight years and had raced in Formula Two. Nonetheless, Mosley is modest about his racing days, saying that his driving does not compare 'with the experience of driving today's state-of-the-art cars that' s a bit like comparing a Battle of Britain Spitfire with a modern-day jet fighter. I have never driven a Formula One car. They cost about £1,000 a mile just to run the engine.'

Mosley often relies on his experience as a barrister when dealing with the people in Formula One and all the other motorsports under FIA authority. He often has to use all his diplomatic skills when bridging the gap between the sensibilities of FIA delegates and the attitudes of racing car drivers.

When Ayrton Senna physically and verbally attacked newcomer Eddie Irvine after his debut for Jordan at the 1993 Japanese grand prix a FIA tribunal was set up. The Irishman had upset the legendary Brazilian by overtaking him even though he was a lap behind. The committee, assembled in Paris to hear the evidence against Senna, was surprised to see Irvine arrive wearing jeans and straight off the plane from the Far East. Members felt he had shown a lack of respect for the proceedings. Mosley explained what happened: 'Ayrton was quite resentful of Irvine and the lack of respect he thought he had shown him. But Irvine's attitude in the tribunal irritated the World Council so much that they all said we should impose a penalty on him. And that's when the lawyer in me surfaced and I had to argue we couldn't do that because he was there as a witness against Senna and he was not the accused. We couldn't fine or punish him for his attitude. That would have been like hanging the chief witness for the prosecution in a criminal trial because the jury didn't like the look of him and letting the culprit off lightly.'

Mosley feels that it is harder to deal with problems caused by teams rather than individuals. He says that it 'is tricky when you get problems with the teams like the difficulty with Benetton at Spa in 1996 when they were disqualified because the engineers got their calculations wrong and were at fault with the crucial thickness of the plank under the car. They got George Carman, one of Britain's leading barristers and a great legal mind, to defend them. He is a very serious lawyer, a genius with a remarkable courtroom presence and with a brilliant record of successes. He was excellent in the World Council. It was a completely foreign and unfamiliar environment to him and he handled it perfectly, very well indeed and it made for some interesting listening a totally fascinating experience for me when he appeared.

'I had never met him, but we have many mutual friends in Lincoln's Inn whom I have known all my life and they all had the same respect and regard for his talent and reputation. He was a really big gun for Benetton and Flavio Briatore to wheel out, just what we would have expected from them under the circumstances.

'I was chairman of the tribunal and, effectively, he was defending counsel. I was in a completely neutral capacity, but had to try and make it all work and run smoothly because the rest of the World Council expect me to know what to do because I am a lawyer.'

Another controversy FIA had to deal with was Michael Schumacher's clash with Jacques Villeneuve at Jerez, Spain, in their showdown European Grand Prix battle in 1997. Schumacher turned his car into Villeneuve's, only to end up with his crippled car stranded in the gravel trap while the French-Canadian kept going and claimed third place and the title. The Ferrari team leader, then paid £1 million per race, refused to apologize to a severely upset Villeneuve. While he was prepared to admit that he had blundered he denied that his actions had been deliberate. The situation caused worldwide uproar with demands for Schumacher to start the following season under at least a ten-point forfeit.

However, after a three-hour disciplinary hearing, Schumacher was punished with little more than community service. He was ordered to tour Southern Europe on FIA's safety campaign to educate motorists in the wearing of seatbelts and his 1997 results were declared void, which meant he lost his second place in the drivers' championship. There was also a general warning that anybody found cheating in the future could expect tough punishment.

Mosley explained the hearing's reasoning, saying, 'There are no set levels of punishment at FIA. There are absolutely no limits to what penalties we can impose, but we strive to make the punishment fit the crime and to be seen to be fair. And the important thing in the Schumacher case was to make sure that drivers were left under no illusion that if you tried to win the championship by taking the other bloke off the track and out of the race as had happened several times in the past, it just was not going to work. You will not succeed because we will take the title off you. That was the chief message.

'Schumacher might well have won the title in 1997 and that would have been Ferrari's dream after such a long spell without it but we would still have cancelled it out. As it was, he was runner-up, but we took that away and his results, brilliant as some of them were, count for nothing for that year. The clear message we wanted to send out to all drivers was: do not try to win unfairly.

'We also considered banning him for three or four races or taking away points for the start of the next season, but I thought that would mess up the 1998 season and punish not only Schumacher and Ferrari but the fans, too. And I reckoned we'd be hitting the fans harder than Michael because we'd be taking the one man out of contention everybody wanted to see. And how would that benefit the sport?

'Another proposal was to fine him heavily with a huge figure maybe $2 million. But that wouldn't have hurt him at all. It's a lot of money, certainly, and that would have been a record fine but it couldn't have troubled him all that much.

'Then there was all the talk and arguments and bad publicity about Bernie Ecclestone's million-pound donation to the Labour Party. It was just starting to be a big issue and we thought we didn't want to fuel people's ideas about the sort of money they imagine is swilling around Formula One. We didn't want people talking money, money, money all the time.'

When the briefly considered and quickly dismissed device of

a fine had been dealt with, Mosley, Ecclestone and the World Council looked for an alternative that was more useful than fiscal. 'That's when the idea of involving him in the road safety campaign came up,' said Mosley. 'OK, I know a lot of critics were disappointed that we didn't punish him with some of the penalties they had suggested, like long bans and the docking of points from the start of the next season, and that using Michael on a road safety issue was like putting a rapist in charge of a girls' school. But I don't see it like that. If you turn up with Mr Nice Guy none of the young men you are trying to influence will be remotely interested. On the other hand, if you arrive with Schumacher, a hero to so many, all the media is going to be there to hear what he's got to say. He explains to them all that he never gets into his Formula One car without putting his seat belt on and they suddenly realize that even Mr Bad does this and far from being uncaring he really is safety conscious.

'Let's be honest, if you run this sort of campaign without somebody like Schumacher it is difficult to get any publicity, any television or newspaper coverage, because it is a subject that is about as absorbing as watching paint drying. So to get Michael involved and he was really up for it was a great way to get some-thing positive out of what could have been a great big negative. And if it helps save just one life then it's all worthwhile but it will save very many lives.'

Nonetheless, many people felt that Schumacher had got off lightly. Indeed, Schumacher's relief at the verdict was little short of ecstatic and he could barely contain his glee after a suitably humble and downcast press conference. There was hardly a mobile telephone in the packed courtyard of the RAC, the scene of the hearing, that wasn't transmitting messages of outrage and surprise at what was thought to have been a mere rapping over the knuckles for a man benefiting from his reputation.

Mosley, to some extent, concurs. He thinks that Schumacher, on hearing the verdict, 'walked out of the room feeling like Houdini. I believe he thought he would be hit by a huge fine on top of his disqualification from the results. Under normal circumstances that's what we would have done, so I believe he walked away feeling really happy and somewhat relieved. I think he had shot himself in the foot in Spain and had damaged himself. But he did say to me that he would have done the safety campaign if we'd asked him, without it being imposed on him. And I think that's probably true.'

Mosley, has also had run-ins with the 1997 world champion, Jacques Villeneuve, particularly following his scathing comments, in 1997, on FIA's proposals of new safety rules and an increase in the number of overtaking opportunities. Mosley denies that he holds any personal animosity towards the French-Canadian, saying, 'I suppose that in most people's minds his is the name that springs to mind when they think I don't like a particular driver. But, in truth, my feeling is exactly the opposite: I like and admire him very much. He is everything a racing driver should be he would never shirk a challenge, the sort of guy who if you said we should have a grand prix round the dodgy old Nurburgring, as it used to be, he'd jump at it. I think that's the right attitude for a racing driver, the restless need to be challenged, fulfilled and victorious in the face of the most daunting challenge. In that case Jacques is certainly the son of his famous father, Gilles. He loved battling the odds and beating them, and it is in the genes.

'When Villeneuve made his stand and offered his opinions about what we were trying to do, it was not so much his attitude, I encourage free speech and expression of views among Formula One drivers, they are welcome when they are constructive, but the manner and, I may say, the language he used. And he certainly wasn't being penalized simply for being outspoken.

'It is not that we have got self-important at FIA: what bothered me and the World Council, was that you get these major companies looking to come into Formula One and spend untold millions of pounds in sponsorships. And, inevitably, you will always have a few in the company who might be against the idea and the investment and are looking for the merest excuse to exercise a veto.

'It is clear to the dumbest person you do not want to allow any doubts to build up that could sabotage the level of investment some of these companies are prepared to go to, and careless talk from drivers of Villeneuve's stature, or anybody else for that matter who is high profile and influential, is sending out the wrong messages and giving the sceptics ammunition. It is like sawing through the branch you are sitting on. You'd be crazy to do it.

'And to be fair, Jacques, who is very bright and intelligent, now understands the point we had to make and I am certain he won't make the same mistake again. His problem was his openness; he said he used to talk to journalists freely like he would to his friends, but you cannot do that.

'When you are as famous as Villeneuve and you apparently have an opinion that is newsworthy they will report it. It is not, however, always to the benefit of our sport and, let's be clear, it damages the interests of the teams and the other drivers.' Furthermore he incurred the wrath of a circle of men with fairly old-fashioned values by using the word 'shit' in his public attack, in relation to the FIA's diligent strivings.

'We simply cannot have that sort of talk', Mosley told me. 'Most of us swear, of course we do, and we use coarse language from time to time but in this context and so publicly, it was out of order.'

Mosley insists that gagging the drivers is not part of FIA's policy, pointing out that it is compulsory for them to give their reaction to the world's media immediately after a grand prix.

FIA's exact powers were clearly explained by Bernie Ecclestone when he said, 'These drivers should understand that there is nothing we cannot do as a means of punishment if they step out of line. We can fine them, ban them and penalize them as we think fit for the greater good and protection of the sport. No matter who they are, how famous or how important they imagine they are. We have the power to take away their liveli-hood. That is why we have a strictly controlled regime where penalties can be punitive and appeals against them, if you lose, even more exacting. Reckless and dangerous driving, unseemly behaviour, anything that brings Formula One into disrepute, we can hit as hard as we like. And I can promise that's the way it will always be.'

Pit-lane speeding, where the driver forgets to activate the limiter as he heads for a fuel stop, can result in a $7,000 fine. Crossing the track during a race, even if a car has broken down right opposite its garage, or forgetting to leave a stranded car in neutral can attract equally stinging fines for the offending drivers and they rarely appeal for fear of an increase of the punishment.

There are also fines for not providing certain media opportunities. The top three finishers must attend a post-race press conference as failure to do so is punishable by a $30,000 fine. Similarly, a non-appearance by any of the top three on the winner's podium, short of them being under medical treatment, will receive a similar punishment. Mosley feels that although the fines are nominal they serve to remind drivers of their duties. He says, 'All of the top drivers could easily pay the fine, but I don't think any of them would not turn up and I can't recall it ever happening because they know, as we all do, that their appearance for the media, and on the podium, is all part of their job. They know everybody's got to work together for the good of Formula One and the journalists, up to 500 of them at any grand prix, depend on the drivers and what they say for their stories. And it is our duty to Formula One to make sure the widest possible interest is maintained and that the facilities to do so are kept monitored and in place.'

While Mosley understands the importance of being media friendly he believes that Formula One can become yet more popular. He says, 'The major success of F1 is that it captures a television audience now we never thought possible in countries which have neither a circuit nor a driver, nothing to give them an identity or a connection with grand prix racing other than a desire to be able to see a great spectacle.

'It is a completely unique phenomenon in world sport because unlike football with its big audience because of its dozens and dozens of matches and the Olympics, every four years, which everybody watches anyway, we have an event that takes place no more frequently than every two weeks but which is watched all over the world on TV by tens of millions of people. And it will only get bigger and better as we expand into other countries and reach untapped sources of support and enthusiasm.

'It would be very easy to mess it all up if we were not careful. Very easy indeed. If we were to divide it up, split it and interfere with it in the wrong way, or do something that spoils it in the way that world boxing, for instance, has been damaged and has been allowed to disintegrate. It really is incredible because a heavyweight championship could be as big as Formula One but the powers concerned with boxing have given us all a clear warning that if you are involved in the management of a major sport and you mess about with it and make mistakes there's no going back.'

During 1997 and 1998, Ecclestone and the teams signed the Concorde Agreement, an arrangement for the teams to work in harmony for the greater good of motor racing. It is hoped that this will help to prevent Formula One disintegrating in the manner of boxing. Mosley explained the motivation for the agreement, saying, 'Sometimes I think teams lose sight of the dangers. They are so engrossed in their own competition with other teams that they ignore the overall picture and the necessity of avoiding making some serious mistake. Bernie Ecclestone plays a crucial role because he sees the bigger picture quite clearly and is conscious of the dangers that can develop. The possible mistake would be some huge conflict in the sport, or dividing it up in some way and getting two rival series rather like boxing has done. That would be a big error because the F1 show is a fine spectacle and it must not be endangered.'

Mosley believes that part of the excitement of Formula One lies in the tactical battles. He says, 'Pit stops, and the strategy surrounding them have enormous interest to the outsiders. My argument is that while the insiders all say there is not enough overtaking, the truth of it for the outsiders is the fascination of the whole sporting picture and not just having five overtaking manoeuvres and a leader change every lap like they do in motorcycle racing.

'I don't think the doubters foresaw how interesting it could all be with the fans going to the pub after a grand prix and discussing and arguing whether a driver should have had two or three pit stops or what tyres he should have been using and that he should have gone that bit quicker at that part of the race because he was on his new tyres. Most of what happens in a Formula One race, the strategy while the cars are on the track, is concealed. It's secret and there is no way of finding out what is going to happen.

'But the entire strategy of a pit stop and the laps that precede and succeed it are obvious and evident to everybody and they can work out for themselves and see what is actually happening in all the drama and excitement and tension of a pit stop taken at the height of the action.'

Despite enjoying the tactical battles of pit stops Mosley is also alive to their dangers. He comments, 'We have seen some of the results when they go wrong. The 1994 Benetton fire at the German Grand Prix at Hockenheim was frightening and could have been much nastier. It was lucky it wasn't any worse thanks to the very prompt reactions of the pit crew.

'Racing by definition produces dangers. And there are arguments amongst the teams against refuelling stops. If you are going to race cars at 200 mph with anything up to forty to fifty gallons of fuel on board there is obviously a big risk. On the other hand, if you don't have pit stops and you start off with fifty gallons of fuel, which is a lot of stored up energy, and you have an accident you could have an enormous fire. The car weighs a lot more so it is much harder to stop if it goes out of control.

'If you have a fire in pit lane, which I realize is a fear, it is potentially very dangerous. But you have all the equipment and properly dressed and expert personnel there to deal with it straight away. And, anyway, I believe the risks of an outbreak have been largely reduced. It may not be too much fun for the pit crews, particularly when it goes wrong, when a wheel nut won't come off or the fuel rig goes wrong and won't feed, or the driver stalls the car, but you cannot deny that it is sheer unadulterated excitement in full colour close-up.'

While Mosley holds the commercial success of Formula One close to his heart, safety is always a key issue. 'The real work of FIA is all to do with the safety of this new car seat, or that crash test, or this new emission control and traffic mobility problem,' he says. 'All the time I am talking to people at the European Union or in America discussing just about every aspect of motoring and striving to bring the industry together worldwide, serving the interests of the ordinary motorist.'

On the commercial side of things Mosley has some interesting views on the fuss made over Bernie Ecclestone's £1 million donation to the Labour party and the Government's attempt to get an exemption from the EU ruling against tobacco advertising in motor racing. Mosley says: 'It was a difficult situation because everybody gets emotional about the cigarette thing. FIA, as such, has nothing to gain one way or the other from tobacco because we do not get any benefit. We are purely involved in trying our best to defend the interests of the teams in F1. I see that as part of our responsibility because there is no doubt we do make a lot of enemies when we defend the teams from the anti-tobacco lobby. That's a great pity because it does prejudice other work which we feel is just as important.

'The unfortunate thing is that it was the Government who put forward this idea of an exemption from tobacco advertising for Formula One. They hadn't asked us and we never asked for it. They just did it without consulting us.

'When they told us, "we're going to go for an exemption for Formula One," I immediately said that whatever you do, don't do that, it is a fundamental error. And they said that it was too late, they had done it. My answer was that they should undo it right away because, first of all, they were going to have all the other sports against us. And my advice was for them to keep it vague and say there would be an exemption for certain major world events. That way, all the other sports would think that as they run major world events it could be them. So you have got them on your side. And, secondly, in the EU, of the fifteen countries only eight have a grand prix, so straight away the others who don't are against you. Whereas if it is a major sport the other seven will all have something they want to do so on both counts it was a fundamental error. That's what really caused all the trouble.

'If it had been done as it should have been done, with an exemption just for the major world events, it would have been much easier to sell in the EU and we would not have caught all the flak we caught here in Britain. But the trouble is everybody is desperate to get things done.

'If the present arrangement on tobacco advertising stands and it goes onto 2006 it is so far in the future it is difficult to tell what will happen and what direction Formula One will take, but there has to be a tendency to (take motor racing) to the Far East. This is not blackmail. We are a sport that can run inside the EU or outside it. If we are deprived of sponsorship worth more than £100 million it is quite obvious we will go elsewhere.'

Mosley, who stopped smoking on health grounds more than thirty years ago, went on: 'We are totally committed to bringing in a voluntary code which will reduce tobacco advertising and we have made it clear that if they deliver an exemption from the EU directive, we will deliver a meaningful code.'

In any case, Mosley would like to see changes in the structure of Formula One whether tobacco advertising is banned or not. He feels that 'we have far too many F1 races in the EU and not enough in the rest of the world, and that I think will eventually be balanced out by increasing, as I would like to see, the number of grands prix to about twenty. The problem is that the teams won't stand for it. I would like to cut down the private testing dramatically and then slash the racing, practice and qualifying programme from Friday, Saturday and Sunday to just Saturday and Sunday. That way you gain sixteen days and use eight of them for four more two-day grands prix and give the other eight days back to the teams. It is a rational way of approaching it, but whether they will all come round to seeing it that way is another matter entirely. It is my view that we could use the increase in GPs to serve Asia without having to cut back on the number of events in Europe. Bernie would like it to happen. At the moment it is the teams that would not but as long as the Concorde Agreement exists FIA cannot make any changes without talking to the teams and getting their co-operation and support.'

The success of Formula One is firmly based on its global appeal and it claims an average of some 320 million viewers in 130 countries for each of its races. That is quite clearly an attractive proposition for the cigarette companies looking for exposure and new markets; any plan to shift the focus of the sport to the Far East, where there is a more ambivalent attitude to advertising, will have irresistible appeal to companies who presently pump around £40 million a year into the leading teams.

The downside is that any move away from Europe would be enormously damaging to the British racing car industry which is worth £1.3 billion. Britain makes about 90 per cent of the world's race and rally cars and exports half its products. Many thousands of jobs would be jeopardized, and that is a serious concern. McLaren, Williams, Stewart and now British American Racing, TWR Arrows, Benetton and Jordan are all based in an area north of London known as 'the Golden Triangle'.

Whatever the future holds for Formula One Mosley could not have a stronger or more influential ally than Bernie Ecclestone. Indeed they form two points of another Formula One triangle, with Mosley as President of FIA, Ecclestone as the commercial rights holder and the teams forming the third point. Mosley explained that, 'Under a previous arrangement FIA would make an agreement with the teams, which in turn would reach an agreement with a commercial rights holder. Now, instead of a straight line, what we have is a triangle: FIA has agreements with both the commercial rights holder and with the teams. Part of each of the agreements provides that the commercial rights holder will pay the teams the monies as laid down in the Concorde Agreement.

Mosley uses one particular example of how the operation works, saying, 'Two or three years ago Mr Ecclestone made an enormous investment in digital television at a time when almost everyone, including the bosses at the top TV companies, were saying it was too much of a gamble and he would lose every penny. And that nobody would pay for something they could get for nothing on terrestrial TV. How wrong. It is now looking as though digital TV is going to be a massive success. That is good for Bernie because he took a huge risk and may now be profiting from it.

'It is even better for the teams, though, because although they took no risk at all, they do not have to meet any of the costs involved and, therefore, they now make an even bigger profit than he does. It is my view that the arrangements are more than fair to the teams.'

Mosley is keen to attribute the commercial success of Formula One to Ecclestone. 'I would suggest that the reason why Formula One makes such good profits is not unassociated with the fact that Bernie in my view is a financial genius and that he works almost twenty-four hours a day making the whole Formula One business succeed,' he says. 'The easiest thing for him to have done would have been to sell the TV rights at minimum cost, employing one secretary and one lawyer, and simply take his percentage, spending as little as possible. Instead, what he has done, is to undertake a huge capital investment, setting up an enormous broadcasting operation, taking on a vast staff and meeting all the costs out of his percentage.'

Mosley is excited about the prospect of using digital TV to cover motor racing. He says, 'As far as digital TV is concerned, we are extremely fortunate to be able to command a mass terrestrial free-over-the-air audience at the same time as having a very successful pay-TV operation. The two complement each other. With football, for example, three different camera angles are not going to help it very much; if you have the opportunity to watch the games free you are unlikely to be prepared to pay money just to watch the same thing from a few alternative camera angles. By contrast, in F1, the pay-TV organizations are being offered the facilities we have at a race track, and once the viewer gets interested in F1, those facilities will generate considerable enthusiasm. Even relatively mildly interested fans will want to have the ability to be able to ride with the leading cars, to see the times come up on the screen and have the section splits put before them just as they are for the driver as he sits in the garage.

'I firmly believe the free-over-the-air TV will continue to grow and have an enormous audience which will continue to generate sponsorship for the teams but there will also be a significant minority which, in fact, is likely to expand because of the mass audience being exposed to the possibilities of pay TV and the availability of digital transmission.

'The top events in almost all sports will offer a choice of either free-to-air or pay-TV and I forecast that on free-to-air television the number of sporting events which rival Formula One will decline and that will benefit F1 as a worldwide top sporting event. Technology has played into our hands.

Mosley would like to see Ecclestone take Formula One to the stock market. He says, 'His company is big and getting bigger and could go public and FIA would welcome that because it would mean that every detail of the finances of F1 would be out in the open and nobody could complain. It would be to the benefit of everybody. We have been going through an entrepreneurial phase, a very brilliant one, which is almost finished and the final stage is the development of pay TV and digital transmission. Whether Bernie then wants to take his company public is entirely a matter for him.'

Of course, even at the moment a huge part of Formula One's income is generated by television. In the TV money split, and the total is a closely guarded secret, it is thought that half the gross figure, whatever the expenditures, goes to the teams in the agreement with any dissidents from the deal receiving nothing.

The complicated system of prize money makes it virtually impossible to quantify exactly how much a team can win, unlike other major sports such as golf and tennis where there are set figures and the rewards are widely publicized. Mosley is happy to explain the system without revealing what every grand prix follower really wants to know, the bottom-line take-home figure. 'The total income is divided up into two equal parts,' he explains. 'The first part is split equally between the signatory teams competing during the entire championship and who have been one of the top ten in two of the previous. The second part is paid to all eligible signatory teams from first to tenth place in the championship. The money gets divided among the top ten teams, with regard to the results of two of the previous three years, any two, and provided they competed in the whole of the immediately preceding championship. The first gets the most, the tenth gets the least.

'But the net result is that the smaller teams do get a great deal more than they ever did before because of a combination of two things. Firstly, they get a bigger percentage, so their share of whatever money is available goes up and, secondly, the money that is available has increased dramatically in 1997 and 1998 compared to previous years because Mr Ecclestone has pulled off such tremendously successful deals with television. ITV, for instance, have paid ten times what the BBC used to pay for the rights to show Formula One. The teams get more or less half of the entire TV income before expenses: all the costs, like Bernie's airliner and whatever other outlay is made, comes out of our part of it.

'It is all a much better and a far more satisfactory arrangement than we used to have. Under the original Concorde Agreement there was an extremely complicated method of splitting up the prize money after each race. Proportions were allocated for grid positions, for the previous year's results and a split of the race prize money according to the teams' positions at quarter-, half- and full-race distance. But all that has now been swept aside.'

Mosley enjoys helping Ecclestone try to widen the appeal of Formula One. Their aim is to present it as a package which can compete with the likes of football for room on the back pages of newspapers. 'We know people now talk about F1 in the pubs and they love to discuss the relative merits of drivers heroes and villains,' says Mosley, 'but it is difficult to get the newspaper coverage on an equal par with, say, football.

'Looking at the TV figures around 1988, 1989 and 1990 they were starting to increase but in 1994 they rocketed. And it was all down to the controversy and the focus F1 was getting with Damon Hill and Schumacher clashing all year and then colliding in Australia, and with Schumacher's disqualification at Silverstone when he ignored a black flag. It was a bonanza. But it only hit me when I was talking to an interviewer and I asked her why she was interested. She told me everybody was talking about the events in the pub. And that, for me, was the answer. You can have the most exciting race ever, full of incident and it's worth about ten minutes' talk in the pub. But get some controversy, like Eric Cantona jumping from the pitch into the crowd and kicking a spectator or a car catching fire, then that's it. You are in business so far as the punter is concerned.'

Mosley recalled another incident that hit the headlines: the incident when Schumacher, whilst driving for Benetton in 1994, ignored the black flag, the signal that a specified car must stop and pull into the pits. 'The reaction of those not involved was as if a footballer had been shown the red card and had more or less told the referee to sod off. And the trainer was standing by the side of the pitch saying, "Don't take any notice, keep playing." The whole authority of the sport was called into question. And we can't have that.'

The subsequent heavy ban on Schumacher, at a time when he was threatening to run away with the championship and wreck it as a contest, was reckoned by a cynical faction to have been a device for FIA to pep up a title chase that was turning into a one-horse race. Mosley responded to the claim by saying, 'The accusation of fixing things for entertainment will always be there but at that stage the championship was wholly unpredictable. Schumacher could have had an accident, broken his arm, anything, and nobody could foresee that Hill would win the two races Schumacher missed, or that Schumacher's engineers would mess up his settings that would lead to his disqualification at the Belgian Grand Prix. Not only that, Hill blew him off fair and square in Japan in the last race but one to set up a finale full of promise.

'It could easily have been another situation entirely, where to suspend somebody could have been a disaster that killed off the championship altogether. As it turned out, it was lucky that we could not have had a better scenario for the last race of the championship, the decider, with maximum public interest.

'Part of the magic and the appeal of Formula One is its unpredictability. You cannot legislate for much of what happens and when you have such a widely differing collection of personalities and clever and talented people intent on giving their all in pursuit of the ultimate prizes in grands prix the result is usually an event and a series to stir the imagination and the memory for many years to come.'

Mosley does not want to see the dangers increased in order to make for a greater spectacle. He explained, 'I recall talking at a briefing in Japan a few years ago and saying that we must avoid wheel-to-wheel contact and that sort of Hollywood *Ben Hur* charioteer stuff ... and a top driver, a guy I respected very much and had known a long time, said to me "You do realize, don't you, that in modern Formula One you more or less can't over-take unless you are prepared to do a bit of wheel banging."'

That succinctly sums up the dilemma that faces Mosley and his watchdogs at FIA: most front-running drivers will always be willing to risk a collision to get to where they want to be. Mosley's attitude is: 'You cannot have rigid rules or tell a driver how to race because if any of us were ever there it was a very long time ago. On the other hand if it gets to be dangerous, you have to stop it.'

RON DENNIS

**Managing Director,
McLaren-Mercedes**

The pristine tidiness and antiseptic orderliness of Ron Dennis's uncluttered desk and his office surroundings are the first clue to his obsessive insistence on precision in everything.

Dennis is a fascinating but enigmatic character, often hiding behind the confusion caused by what is known around Formula One as 'Ronspeak' his sometimes impenetrable way with words. He is, and has been for a long time, one of the most intriguing figures in Formula One. He is not always the most popular man in the sport, but which eminently successful and fabulously wealthy person ever is?

The evidence of his global success glitters and gleams in the thirty-metre long, floor-to-ceiling trophy cabinet at the McLaren headquarters near Woking in Surrey.

Dennis is aware of the popular view that he is a very cold man and is happy to admit that there is some truth in it. 'I am knowingly devoid of emotion during the grand prix weekend, but it comes for two reasons,' he says. 'First of all I try to be focused. And my level of focus, I think, is pretty high. Secondly, I see emotion as a weakness and not a strength … If you can control your emotions by being cool, calm and collected, and it is not by accident that cool, calm and collected are all together, you will shape your own destiny from the basis of a firm mindset.

'I am there to do a job. I am there to demonstrate by example to people in the team that if you are focused and you are disciplined, and that doesn't mean to say I can't give a humorous line and that I can't laugh or smile, it is the right way to be.'

Dennis was a close friend of Ayrton Senna, the Brazilian racing genius who was killed at Imola on lap seven of the San Marino Grand Prix in 1994. It is perhaps in his reaction to the tragedy that Dennis's character is revealed: he suffers the same emotions as the rest of us but does not openly display them. 'He was a particular friend but I didn't cry when he was killed because that wasn't the right emotion,' he said. 'You know and understand pain as an adult and as a grown-up you don't cry. You cry when you are a child and you have pain, but as an adult the sort of pain you get when a good friend dies does not make you weep.'

Interestingly, the time when Dennis is unable to control his emotion is when he achieves the professional success he is so hungry for. 'There was for me a massive release when we won our first race for ages, when David Coulthard won in Australia in March 1997,' he says. 'That, I have to confess, was a real rush and it was so emotional it caught me out. It pulled out a plug I didn't realize was there and the emotion came flooding out; I was pretty watery I can tell you, but I managed to control it so it wasn't picked up on camera and I was quite pleased and relieved about that.'

Apart from 'Ronspeak', Dennis is also capable of being extremely blunt. One of the more colourful and memorable phrases attributed to him came when Eddie Jordan, who had given Michael Schumacher his first chance in Formula One in 1991, lost the promising young German newcomer to Benetton, having been outwitted by Flavio Briatore. 'Welcome to the Piranha Club,' said Dennis to the anguished and bitterly disappointed Jordan.

He holds the same view of Formula One now, believing that its machinations, backtracking and double-dealing are analogous to a Piranha Club where the weak and the unwary would be ruthlessly gobbled up. He explained: 'If you are in Formula One and you are not a competitive individual, and I mean anywhere in F1, you are really going to struggle and have a tough time ... It is a cut-and-thrust business where the rewards for success are massive and the penalties for failure are punitive. When you go into a grand prix environment you are constantly trying to out-manoeuvre and out-think your opposition and I don't mean only in how you are going to run the car in such a way that you win. I am talking about every single aspect of grand prix racing: the politics, the sponsorships, the way you portray yourself, how you race, how you look, how you attract investment and how you optimize or shape your performance.

'You can conceptualize that it is like being in a tank of piranhas. Let's say one of these piranhas snaps at a tail by accident and suddenly one fish weakens. The rest of them have got to decide whether they eat it up or hold back.'

Dennis then adds, 'If I were swimming around in a tank with Frank Williams and Ken Tyrrell I would feel a lot more secure than I would be with other Formula One colleagues who shall remain nameless.' It is perhaps surprising that Dennis would openly endorse two rival team owners in such a competitive sport. But Formula One is also a business and the three had joined forces in the long-running dispute with Max Mosley and Bernie Ecclestone, the president and vice-president of FIA, about such issues as the division of TV money.

Dennis likes to be in control. He will not, for instance, allow even senior management level people to make comment and give media interviews, even though they are not intended to be contentious, without his prior permission but a request more often than not carries a veto. There are many stories about his perfectionist nature. He once binned thousands of pounds worth of designer suede jackets meant for the team until he found a flaw; he ripped up and replaced his gravel drive at home because it had become grubby; he has ceramic flooring laid down in the garage before every grand prix.

The perfectionist's attention to the most minor detail holds him in good stead when negotiating a driver's contract. However, he did once break with tradition when he clashed with an equally unbending negotiator, Ayrton Senna, to thrash out the details of an extension on the Brazilian driver's contract. They reached a stalemate and Dennis's solution was to toss a coin. Senna called correctly and Dennis gave way.

Although Dennis's dedication takes the team a long way he recognizes that he needs talented people around him. He also accepts that if you want the best, you have to buy the best. That's how he persuaded Formula One's most brilliant aerodynamics expert, Adrian Newey, to join McLaren-Mercedes. Newey had formerly been with Williams where his cars had won championships for Nigel Mansell, Alain Prost, Damon Hill and Jacques Villeneuve. His McLaren cars for 1998 soon became championship pacemakers for Mika Hakkinen and David Coulthard and Newey, who was granted a greater depth of authority than he had been allowed at Williams, proved to be worth every penny of his reported £2 million wages.

Dennis's attempt to persuade 1996 world champion Damon Hill to join McLaren from TWR Arrows, where he was having a disastrous time, halfway through the 1997 season, is another example of the McLaren manager's quest for the best. The deal, however, foundered on Hill's insistence on a flat fee rather than a performance-related bonus plan. But it wasn't Dennis who came off worst, as subsequent results have indicated. Bernie Ecclestone believed that Hill should have accepted the offer, commenting, 'Damon was a very silly boy and, perhaps, he was badly advised. But if he had taken the McLaren offer, whatever it was, he could surely have trebled the money he was getting at Jordan and, I am sure, he would have won the championship again. It was obvious to everybody that the car, particularly on the Bridgestone tyres, was going to be an absolute winner.'

Dennis is happy to explain what happened in his attempts to sign the Englishman and why he tried to do so. 'We were never in a position to decide on him because he withdrew from discussions which had within them "If we do this, what's your reaction?",' he says. 'And the reaction was, "Well, if you do that, I am not interested." It was fine by me. I was comfortable with the results that came out of those discussions. We are an English team, based in England, and Damon is an English driver, a good one and a former world champion. The obvious desire of the customer, the television and the media, would have been to see him having a good drive, that's why I had discussions with him about joining us.'

Even without Hill, Dennis was still able to put two very competent drivers in his cars: Mika Hakkinen and David Coulthard. Neither Hakkinen nor Coulthard suffered any similar qualms when Dennis took them individually into the McLaren motorhome and outlined similar contracts to the one offered to Hill.

Another example of Dennis's keenness to be surrounded by the best available team was his attempts to get Michael Schumacher to join McLaren. He was left bemused by the German's decision to join Ferrari, saying, 'You don't need to be Einstein to realize that Michael Schumacher driving for Ferrari just does not seem logical if winning is the objective.' He must have wished that he could eat his words when Schumacher's winning streak pulled Ferrari level on points with only two races to go.

Schumacher's decision sabotaged Dennis's ambition to have, as with three-time champion Senna, or four-time champion Alain Prost, the best driver of the age in one of his cars. Any driver who can compensate with outright skill and daring for the deficiencies of a car, as Schumacher had done at both Benetton and at Ferrari, is rightly regarded as a treasure. It is easy to imagine that the German would have run away with the 1998 championship had he been in the McLaren-Mercedes. The McLarens are regarded as the best cars, Schumacher the best driver.

Dennis's account of his endeavours to sign Schumacher give a riveting insight into the complexities of driver transfers and the problems of having to deal with so many different people. 'Most drivers have managers and those managers have different styles of approach and negotiation,' he says. 'Sometimes you think that the motivation of one specific manager is more to satisfy their own financial aspirations rather than ensure that their driver is placed in the best environment in which he could perform to his optimum level.

'The main difference between drivers is their own perception of what a team can or cannot do. When I reflect on the initial discussions I have had with a variety of drivers (including Schumacher), I can look back and say in every single instance you go through a process where there are all sorts of walls you have to break down in order to get to the point where you have meaningful dialogue. And that is something I have never had with Michael Schumacher.

'I have never really achieved that with Michael because he has always had a single-mindedness about him and I don't think he has ever really fully exploited his options. He has always taken the view, and instructed those people who represent him, to achieve a certain objective and a certain bargain and has then left them to get on with it. Then there is what I call the Ferrari factor and that is that every driver who goes there does it in the belief that the team can fix the missing link in his life.'

Apart from the difficulties of trying to attract drivers to the team the manager also has to make sure that his current drivers do not lose his trust. 'What we decided to do was to tell both Mika and David that we were evaluating all our options so that we did not put them under any pressure,' Dennis explains. 'We wanted to be professional and not destabilize them. I said to them, "Look, we are going to go through this process. Try and understand. We are a grand prix team and anything we feel we can take as a decision to enhance our chances of winning, whether it is about changing drivers or anything else, then we are going to take it."

'It was no reflection on their ability. I was merely examining the options, making sure they knew what was going on, and striving to do what I thought might be best for McLaren-Mercedes. I was at pains to explain to them there are no holy cows and my own job is only as secure as my competence.'

After the 1998 German Grand Prix at Hockenheim Dennis extended the contracts of Hakkinen and Coulthard. It seemed that he was now convinced there was no need for him to chase other drivers when he endorsed the pair by saying, 'The team spirit and consistency of both Mika and David has played a key part in our decision. We are fortunate to have two top drivers at McLaren and there is every indication that they can only get better and better.'

Dennis has not always been successful in his driver alliances, however. The signing of 1994 world champion Nigel Mansell to drive a McLaren that was revolutionary in its clumsy mid-wings design but also unattractive and ineffective is a case in point

The two had had their differences in the past, but when the forty-one-year-old Mansell agreed to join McLaren, in 1995, Dennis was pleased to have signed such a high-profile driver at a time when his team was struggling, even at a price of £3 million.

However, it was not long before Mansell found he could not fit into the car. His stocky bulk, the size of his backside and the narrowness of the McLaren and its cramped cockpit conspired to make it an ill-fitting missile for the returning race hero. After manfully trying to come to terms with the difficulties, he finally parked the wayward McLaren by the side of the track in Spain in 1995. The one-time F1 and IndyCar champion never raced a Formula One car again.

At the time Dennis explained what went wrong by saying, 'In different circumstances perhaps Nigel could have done a better job for the team and we a better job for him. But that is not what developed following the initial running of the car. I think the thing that both he and the team concluded was that the performance of the team and the car needed to be right for him to give 100 per cent. Otherwise, he wouldn't really be honest to himself or the team and in those circumstances it was better not to continue the relationship. It's as simple as that.'

In 1998 Dennis still regrets the debacle. He now says, 'With Nigel we were very specific about what we were trying to achieve together. It was very carefully planned out. But we were caught out because we fixed the specification of the car before he had a chance to drive it. And until he actually got behind the wheel we didn't realize the car was too small for him that was embarrassing for us, though there was a reason. We had designed the car for a smaller bottom and narrower hips. Once we had eliminated that problem by building some new chassis we arrived at a point where I said, "It isn't working for me, is it working for you?" Nigel's response was, "It's certainly not working for me, is it working for you?"

'At that point we had an extremely amicable parting. He had wanted to get into a car which would win races and carry him to

141

the championship again. We weren't then in a position to provide him with that opportunity. It was like the old McLaren driver John Watson situation. I am sure he'd have won a world championship if he had been in the right car, he was good enough. But motor racing is about being in the right place at the right time ... and neither he nor Mansell were in our case.'

Many people in Formula One think that Dennis likes his drivers to conform to a certain image while they need the ability to win a race they should also enjoy athletic looks, be almost old-fashioned in their good manners and be intelligent; in other words, they should be conventional. 'I can understand the perception,' says Dennis. 'And I think the answer is that the guys who can win grands prix and are really committed to being a Formula One success do not need the avant garde approach that some of the other less talented drivers need to provide them with alternative media perception.

'There was a guy, a small Italian driver who used to drive for Ferrari and a couple of other teams, who used to wear a cowboy hat and always used to have his hair somewhere down around his shoulders. And I thought if a guy needs to try that hard to make some sort of statement then it demonstrates to me a severe problem of insecurity.

'It is not the need to conform, it is nothing to do with that. (It is) more to do with common sense because surely it is eminently more practical when you stick a crash helmet on your head to have short hair. And it is eminently more desirable if you are a human being to keep yourself clean and tidy because the alternative is dirty and dirty smells. And that is not a particularly pleasant environment for him or anybody else around him. So logic dictates that a guy who is really committed and focused and has all the ingredients that you as a team owner consider necessary to succeed and to look good and sound sensible while he is doing it must be the preferable option. And if that is what is perceived as a McLaren type, then it is OK by me.'

Whatever the problems McLaren have had in the past, the team certainly hit the ground running at the start of the 1998 season, lapping the entire field in the first race. It was as though all the other grand prix teams had hibernated through the winter lay-off and left it to the Woking outfit to get on with developing a car that could win the championship. A few races had gone by before Michael Schumacher and Ferrari were able to offer some competition.

Dennis attributes McLaren's newfound success to several factors but accepts that Adrian Newey must take some credit. He says, 'The performance of the team had started to improve in 1997 and Adrian would be the first to recognize that there were some good things happening which he then supplemented and optimized. He certainly brought his further expertise into specific areas and increased the momentum at which we were going up.

The McLaren-Mercedes manager believes that the ethos of the people involved has also been a crucial factor. 'It's a team now and we all subscribe to it,' he says. 'The key is that we build on what we have and ensure that we keep it going. We are on a treadmill and you have to keep people focused and ambitious and as determined as the next man to keep it turning. But, having said that, you have to make it as nice an experience as you can and make sure people get time off, get some home life.

So the system has to give something back, it has to let them have a degree of normality. Not like the old days when people would come from, say Australia and New Zealand, and dedicate five years of their life to Formula One and the people who were running the race teams would exploit the hell out of them, their enthusiasm, their commitment and just about everything else. It was like cheap labour. It's different nowadays we want to make sure people have as normal a life as possible outside the racing environment.

'It may have done the job ten or fifteen years ago when people were perhaps more vulnerable to exploitation, but now you have got to rotate people: to use a soccer analogy, there has to be a squad that is greater in number than the players you actually put on the pitch at any one time. And you have to have a deep understanding of human resource and how to get the fullest benefits without killing the interest and focus of the people who work for your team.

Dennis believes that the success of the team is not because they have an extra ingredient but because they have the right balance of ingredients. 'As for catching the rest of the grid napping, people will always look for an ingredient which they themselves don't have because they cannot come to terms with the fact they are not achieving,' he says. 'If you've got a widget and nobody else has got it, it is simply that. You have it. They don't.

'That was very much the reason why we voluntarily took off our new braking system in Brazil. Everybody else said the system, which they hadn't thought of or developed, was why we were winning races. So we took it off and proceeded to virtually lap the field at Interlagos.

'The real reason for the team's emergence into competitiveness was a direct result of a feeling right through the team that we wanted to be winners. If you are going down, and companies can do that, are you going to pull back and go back up again? It's up to you. Even the biggest companies, for some reason, can have some pretty difficult troughs, but if you have depth, if you have strength, then you are going to climb out of it, you are going to come back and be successful.

'It's like that with grand prix racing. It's a sport, but let's remember it is a business, too. And from a business perspective it responds very well indeed to hard work, focus and discipline.'

Although he is too modest to say so, part of the team's success must be attributed to Dennis himself. His will to win rubs off on his staff. 'The question is: do we want to be failures, do we not want to succeed?, he says. 'My answer is: I don't want to be classed as a failure. It is a word not in my dictionary. So I try to show everybody else.'

It is this attitude that has helped to make McLaren-Mercedes such a major force in 1998.

THE DRIVERS

**Michael Schumacher, Damon Hill
and David Coulthard**

Michael Schumacher

There is a degree of paranoia among Formula One drivers. Throughout their racing infancy they worry they are not good enough to get to the top. When they eventually make it to the grid they worry that they are not good enough to stay there. When they have finally proved themselves as drivers they worry that their sublime talent is not being properly valued or financially recompensed.

In contrast, Michael Schumacher, universally regarded as the finest driver of his generation and arguably even better than Ayrton Senna at his best, can command a vast salary because he is in a class of his own. Eddie Irvine explains his Ferrari team-mate's earning power by saying: 'Michael is on another planet from the rest of us. He can fashion a win from a no-chance-at-all situation. When it all goes right for him and the car is as good as he wants it to be there is one race for him and another one for everybody else on the grid. We are lucky if we see him again after the start. He's got the cake. We are left to scratch around for the crumbs.' Damon Hill was able to rival Schumacher when he was driving the supreme Williams-Renault car and Schumacher was struggling with a wayward Benetton, but even Hill is in awe of Schumacher, saying simply, 'He's like Superman.'

The German has, however, been called other names in his ruthless and sometimes reckless pursuit of ultimate grand prix glory. He has been banned, fined, disqualified and was even excluded from second place in the 1997 championships. He has also been reviled by his peers who have raged about the tactics that have sent them hurtling into the gravel traps or the barriers.

It was ironic that the driver who had caused so much controversy, particularly in critical championship-deciding collisions, either by accident or design, first with Hill in 1994 and then with Villeneuve in 1997, should himself be the enraged victim when he was leading the Belgian Grand Prix in 1998 until he ran destructively into the back of David Coulthard's slowing McLaren on a Spa-Francorchamps circuit rendered treacherous by a downpour and which, in places, offered zero visibility. After the collision he angrily shouldered his way past his own vainly restraining team officials and mechanics to confront Coulthard in the McLaren garage. He accused Coulthard of nearly killing him and deliberately taking him out before he was hustled away, probably to save him from the six-foot Scot who under less provocation had allegedly once threatened 'to slap' Damon Hill.

In many ways it was a sweet moment for those who have suffered at Schumacher's hands over the years he clearly found the same medicine tough to swallow. Schumacher, however, has a different opinion of his driving style. He says: 'I race hard but fair. And I guess other drivers would agree with me. I did cause some aggravation among the more senior drivers like Mansell and Senna when I first came into Formula One, but then they came to respect me for what I was trying to achieve in the car.'

Despite the Ferrari man's anger there was no question that

Junior karter David Coulthard in 1987, aged sixteen. (Above)

Vauxhall-Lotus Champion, 1990. (Right)

David Coulthard locks up on his way to a win at the Portuguese Grand Prix, 1995. (Below)

The Grand Prix
Great off-duty.

Coulthard tests the Benetton-Ford V8 for the
first time, December 1992. (Opposite inset)

The McLaren team celebrate their first win in
50 Grand Prix and after 4 years, at the
Australian Grand Prix, 1997. (Opposite)

Graham Hill and his son Damon in his first racing car, 1964. (Above)

Coulthard celebrates first place at the San Marino Grand Prix with Mercedes-Mclaren 1998. (Opposite)

Damon Hill in Pau with Middlebridge Racing, 1990. (Below)

Damon Hill and Ayrton Senna at the Portuguese Grand Prix, 1994. (Above)

The World Formula One Champion at the Japanese Grand Prix, 1996. (Right)

Hill has a dramatic roll in his Williams Renault during qualifying at the Portuguese Grand Prix, 1994. (Below)

Damon Hill settles to the job of testing the newly launched Arrows Grand Prix A18. (Above)

Testing the Jordan Mugen Honda in Barcelona, 1998.

Hill celebrates his victory and the first Jordan Grand Prix win, 1998. (Above)

The Hill family. (Below)

the collision in the Belgian Grand Prix had been a genuine accident, due largely to Schumacher's carelessness rather than any underhand tactics by Coulthard, as fair and honourable a man as you could hope to find. The Scot was absolved from any culpability by the stewards when it was shown that he had simply been obeying radioed team orders from Ron Dennis to pull over and let Schumacher past. Telemetric and radio-tape evidence proved this to be the case.

The Belgian Grand Prix once again, had proved to be a turning point in Schumacher's career. He went to Spa as its master, with three successive wins at the track he considers his home ground he was born just across the German border in Kerpen and a fourth would have given him the championship lead by three points with only three races to go. He would have already attained four victories but although he finished ahead of the field in 1994 he was sensationally disqualified for the technical infringement of excess wear on the wooden skidblock under his Benetton.

Having bought his first grand prix drive with Dubliner Eddie Jordan's team in 1991 for £150,000 Schumacher will go into the millennium as one of world sport's biggest money spinners after earning £100 million from racing alone. The smallest patch on his blaze-red overalls sets a sponsor back at least £500,000; to buy space on his overalls and cap or his helmet £5 million or more. His merchandising business is also a great success, with a turnover of £70 million in 1998. He could be making still more money but Willi Weber forced him to cut back on the personal appearances where he could make £75,000 by just opening a garage or turning up for an after-lunch speech. The gravy train, ruled his manager, had to have its brakes applied, particularly if it was loaded with only comparatively small beer. Not even Senna with his massive National Bank of Brazil private sponsorship, eclectic financial backing and marketing appeal could compare with the Schumacher business phenomenon once it had started rolling.

It is intriguing to compare the merits of Schumacher and Senna. Schumacher can get the maximum out of any car, how ever deficient mechanically or down on power and handling it might be, and still win or threaten strongly as a potential winner. Senna, on the other hand, may have been a spirited and deadly determined performer his actions sometimes bordering on bullying but the McLaren cars he drove to three world championships were the best in the competition. It is also worth noting that when Schumacher clinched his first Formula One title in 1994 he had only won two grands prix before the season started and was driving a far from reliable Benetton car.

Pat Symonds, who was engineer to both Senna in his formative racing years and to Schumacher in his early days at Benetton is in a unique position to make a considered judgement on their relative qualities. He says, 'They were both drivers clearly talented enough to outclass most of the rest. But even Senna was never as clever as Schumacher at the same age. He was not quite so capable of grasping the detail.

'When Michael first started he used to make silly mistakes, he would over-rev the engine on the first lap. Then we realized he only knew one way to drive: flat out. It wasn't that he was being flash, it was just his style to go as fast as he could from the start. With Senna you could tell him he was far enough ahead and he could coast. Try to tell that to Michael and it would be pointless.

'As people to know off the track they were different, too. Ayrton was cold and clinical, very focused on racing a little bit too much maybe. Michael is far more balanced and a much more rounded man. When we were away from the track, having a meal, he loved to talk about his family or ask about my kids and you always had the impression that if he was not doing what he did and happened to be the guy with an ordinary job living next door, he could become a good mate.

'Michael has it in him to be ruthless and he will not suffer fools. He has the ability to reach down inside himself and produce the streak is necessary. And whatever your job when you are around him you had better do it right.

'Every driver in Formula One is capable of performing to a level beyond our comprehension, but not more than one or two have the intelligence to become world champion. From the first day Michael had a staggering curiosity and an ability to learn That is why he will be champion many times over.'

When asked if it was his ruthlessness that set him apart Schumacher parried the question, answering, 'You must always do what must be done but in a proper way. And always be honest. Then it is not ruthlessness, it is efficiency.' It is interesting to consider how that philosophy would be regarded by some of Schumacher's racetrack victims.

Niki Lauda, the three times Formula One champion who acts as a spare-time adviser to Ferrari also favours Schumacher. He says, 'There have been many great drivers in the past but nobody got to the top as quickly as Michael. We all know what a fantastic driver Senna was, but it took him much longer to reach that level of performance and consistency. Schumacher is incredible. He was outstanding from his first day in Formula One and he climbed the ladder straight away. He is not only fast, but he makes so few mistakes compared with other drivers and far fewer than Senna did when he was a developing young driver. It is my belief that Michael could be the greatest grand prix talent in history.'

Martin Brundle, Schumacher's Benetton partner for two years is another fan. He said of his erstwhile teammate, 'It took me a little time to accept that Michael was so quick, but I had to, and once I did it was no problem for me. The guy is awesome. He is mature beyond his years. It is evident when he is in the car and when he is out of it. He is good in qualifying, he is brilliant in the race, he's fit and determined and he has the stamina and reliability that we all crave. He is going to win lots of races and championships and make an absolute fortune.' When Brundle was reminded of his prediction four years later he said: 'I was wrong. He is even better than I said he was going to be and richer.'

Jackie Stewart, who found himself priced out of the Schumacher bidding when he fired up his Stewart Racing Team with £250 million of Ford backing, also rates Schumacher very highly but he adds a note of caution to the general praise, 'He has become the natural successor to Senna, he is the king, he is now the man to beat. But if he is not careful he could become a spoiled boy,' says Stewart. 'He has missed out in learning how to be important, how to deal with his new-found fame and adulation. And I don't think he is dealing with that as well as he might. There is, as he will learn, much more to being a successful racing driver than just steering the car across the line to victory. But if he does have any weaknesses there are not many showing, none that I can see and I've been around racing a long time.'

Unsurprisingly, Schumacher's manager is another big fan. Willi Weber said of his man: 'On the grand prix grid they are all great drivers the most talented in the world with the finest machinery that costs hundreds of millions of dollars. They all share a common ambition to win, to be the best. They all dream, they all take risks and are happy to do so. And they pray for luck, that little bit of extra that will help. But they all know that to be the champion is to win the lottery. The difference between Michael and the rest of the drivers is that he goes out every day and buys all the tickets.'

Schumacher learnt the rudiments of racing at his father's kart circuit. 'When I knew I had the ability I maybe thought I would be a kart racing professional,' he says. 'The year after I had won the German and European championship I got an offer to race karts for money and that was unusual in that sport. But then I was offered a chance of a Formula Ford test and that's how it all started. I had been warned that kart racers sometimes do not adapt themselves too easily to Formula Ford 1600s but I was on the pace straight away. Inside twenty-five laps I was 2.5 seconds quicker than a guy who was very fast and who had raced against Keke Rosberg before he became world champion. It was the same when I moved into Formula Three. I did about fifteen laps and was more than two seconds faster than the original driver of the car I was in. I would have been on pole for the category.

'But once I had grown used to the idea, when I got older, that

I did have some talent and that it could be the most important factor in my life, I realized I wanted to learn as much as I could about everything: how to dress; how to speak properly; the right things to say; when to shut up and stay quiet; to learn English; and look the part outside the car as well as behind the wheel. I figured there was a lot more to being a racing driver at the very highest level, and a lot more expectation of you from people who mattered, than just being able to go faster than anybody else. Once I had got those ideas firmly placed in my head I dedicated myself to becoming like a sponge that soaked up everything.'

Schumacher's motivation on the track is to do the best that he possibly can. 'I hate not being in a position where I can do something to influence the outcome of a race. That's why I am, I suppose, regarded as a perfectionist,' he says. 'I like to think the car I have to drive is the best one the engineers can produce. Then it is up to me to play my part, to try and turn it into a race-winning car. We all have equal responsibility, whether it is me behind the wheel or the guys behind the wheel nuts when I make a pit stop. If you don't finish a race you cannot win. And we all have to work our hardest to make sure the car has the best chance it can get. My promise is always that I will give it everything I've got. They knew that at Benetton and they know it at Ferrari.

Schumacher then explained his attitude to the dangers of motor racing, saying, 'Do I know fear? Of course I do. Every driver does. But I have supreme confidence in my own ability in the car whether the track is wet or dry. You learn in karting to cope and adapt pretty quickly, particularly in the rain. That is not to say accidents over which you have no control cannot happen. But check my record; you will see that compared with other drivers I have very few crashes. The reason? I respect the circuits. And I am not brainless in the car.

'I judge my limits extremely carefully and I, more than anybody, realize what they are. They may be a little different from those of other drivers maybe there are other guys who take more risks or those who won't take any. I am somewhere in between. But if the car is difficult to drive I will do whatever is necessary. I will find a way around the problem. Maybe I start at 95 per cent and the others at 80 per cent. All the time I am looking for perfection, not just in the way I drive the car, in everything off the track as well. Of course, the excitement in winning and doing it in style against the world's greatest drivers is a fantastic buzz. Once I am on the grid, focused and committed in my mind, I am out there to beat whoever else is alongside me and I think other drivers respect me for what I try to do.'

Schumacher's instinct for self-preservation nearly let him down once, when he was on holiday in 1995. It was an experience he finds impossible to forget and it has left him mentally scarred. On a diving expedition off the coast of Brazil with friends he surfaced to discover that the escort boat had drifted out of sight. Schumacher said of the drama, 'I have never been in a situation where I relied upon somebody else's help in a life-or-death situation. It was the scariest moment of my life.' His companions were exhausted and trod water while Schumacher swam off in search of the boat that turned out to be behind a headland. Fortunately, he managed to reach safety before his reserves of strength and fitness were exhausted. 'Driving cars and going into a corner at 300 kilometres an hour means nothing to me and it represents no threat because I have complete control,' said the Ferrari ace. 'But in the sea in those circumstances you are helpless and you need assistance. I can honestly say I have never been frightened in a racing car because I have confidence in my ability to cope with whatever situation might develop otherwise I could not do my job. And when I do have an accident, which is inevitable in this job, the first thing I worry about is whether the car has been damaged. When I was in the sea I felt just like those people you see in the movies when they are convinced that their life is over. But I was not going to give up.'

In common with other drivers, his feelings about death and its ever-present threat in a business where you drive at 200 mph are usually kept to himself. But he recalls that when Ayrton Senna was killed when his helmet was speared by a suspension strut after his 190 mph crash at the San Marino Grand Prix in 1994 the effect on him was huge. 'When Ayrton died a lot of people imagined it didn't affect me because of the way I went on to win the race,' he says. 'But I had a job to do and I concentrated hard on doing it to the best of my ability, how ever sad the circumstances. Outside that the effect on me was serious. For the first time in my career I had to contemplate death and that it could happen. I certainly hadn't considered it before but I thought about it a lot after Senna was killed. I knew the danger existed, of course. But it was unreal to me that he had gone. I did not believe a top driver like him, the best, could ever be killed. It woke me up to reality. When I first came into Formula One there was no danger for me but now I see a lot more risk and I work to minimize it as much as I can. Sure, I get paid a lot of money for what I do and there are people who would say it is too much but I earn every single penny because I accept the dangers and put my own life on the line to give every bit of effort I can to the team.'

Schumacher is fortunate that those close to him do not worry about his safety. He says, 'There is no pressure on me, only support. And why should I ask for anybody's views? What for? Only a driver can experience the feeling, so what value or use is anybody else's feelings or opinion?'

Schumacher believes he is able to generate so much speed because he is 'as mentally and as physically attuned as it is possible to be'. He says, 'From the moment I get into the car I think about what I am doing. I set my mind and concentrate and try never to look nervous which I am not anyway. I know I am on my own. Basically my technique is to try to get used to whatever situation as quickly as I can. I am prepared for the fight. I know nobody can help me and that crucial decisions will have to be made in a split second at 300 kilometres an hour. I don't need to run myself in to a lap or work up any momentum and I am just as capable of putting in a quick time on the first as I am on the last lap. Some people pick up ten seconds from their first lap to the last whereas I may pick up only one or two seconds. It is difficult to explain, but I am always closer to my limit, even when I start, than most other drivers.

Schumacher feels that another reason why he his able to find a little bit more than other drivers is his understanding of the car. 'It is essential to be able to feel, almost like an instinct, where the limit lies with the car,' he says. 'Then I try to pinpoint what I can do that the others can't or don't do. You have to be able to use your natural instinct, to convert that instinct through your own ability to get 100 per cent out of it, not just once or twice on a lap but all the time. Some drivers may have a better-developed sense for the feel of the car than others and are therefore able to maximize and drive for the maximum time on the limit. They get all that there is to get out of the car. I like to think I am in that category. It is, for me, what makes the difference between a winner and a loser. A car so beautifully and perfectly made by such clever men that can give so much deserves a driver who can use it.'

While the car may be perfectly made racing it still provides a terrific challenge. 'There are messages coming at your brain all the time: sights, sensations, feel, changes,' says Schumacher. 'They all have to be calculated and acted upon. It all sounds crazy and quite frantic to have to do this while you are steering the car and changing gear and watching out for the other guys who all want to win just as badly as you do, but as a racing driver you learn to cope with it as part of the job. When you have done 100 or so grands prix the experience you have amassed helps you develop this sort of mental calculator process and you react quicker to situations because you are identifying problems almost before they arise.'

Schumacher's painstaking determination to be champion means that he accepts sacrifice as the norm and sees success as his just reward. An essential part of his work is an Olympian-style fitness regime. He honed his ten-stone frame to levels way beyond those reached by other drivers until, one by one, they tumbled to his secret and set about catching him up. Despite the efforts of his competitors Jackie Stewart says of Schumacher, 'He is the fittest driver ever in Formula One.' Schumacher himself admits, 'I do work hard at my fitness levels. They are vital to me. And I consider five hours' work in the gym a small price to pay for all the money I am paid to race. Remember, unlike most of the other guys on the grid I am expected to be a winner all the time. I cannot leave anything to chance and being fitter than anybody else is part of the job, like good eyesight, good co-ordination and reflexes. It is the one aspect that you can work on to improve. I try to give my best in every way and that means being super-fit. For me, that is part of the job. These days grand prix drivers have to be able to cope with massive G-forces. Not even top gun jet pilots experience them as much as we do for such long spells and if you are slightly less than at your fittest to handle the demands then you can be in big trouble. It has never happened to me. I have never finished a race feeling washed out. I like to think that no other driver in Formula One is in as good a condition as I am that's why I always look so fresh and so good even after the toughest race in the worst conditions. It gives me an advantage and anything that does that, anything that can help cut even milli-seconds off a lap time, is worthwhile.'

Aside from a gruelling exercise ritual Schumacher has a year-round diet prepared by a fitness expert who travels to all the race and test sessions. The diet, which keeps him in good shape throughout the year, is stricter over the four days at a grand prix when it goes as follows: 8 a.m. tea sweetened with honey. 9 a.m. home-made muesli with natural yoghurt. Noon, after practice, needle pasta, broccoli and a mixed salad with oil plus a Vitamin C capsule. One hour before the race a single muesli bar, as many sips as he likes of tea, apple juice, non-carbonated water or isotonic soft drinks. A tube from another half-litre bottle of specially prepared energy liquid bolted into the cockpit supplies him throughout the race. After the race an early evening meal of chicken, mixed vegetables and corn and soya cakes. 'And a lot of talk about the race,' says Schumacher. 'Then I get home just as fast as I can.'

When Schumacher is in relaxed mood it is difficult to link his smooth urbanity, and what can be infinite charm, with the arrogance he displayed when first became famous. It is not possible to imagine him saying 'Don't you know who I am?' as he did when he was asked politely not to walk through a hotel foyer in South Africa in his swimming trunks. Equally, it is hard to imagine him dismissing Damon Hill's title triumph by saying, 'Well, I'll lend it to him for a year then I will take it back.'

Although his new-found fame made him appear brash it also had another downside. When his celebrity status made it uncomfortable for him to walk his three dogs or go to the supermarket he fled his Monaco home, a grand prix ghetto with at least a dozen Formula One drivers living in the principality, to go and live in an isolated villa on the shores of Lake Geneva in Switzerland. 'He couldn't go anywhere without somebody sticking a camera or a video in his face,' said a friend, 'so he decided to go and live in Switzerland for a bit of peace and quiet.' Schumacher explained, 'I know I am to a large extent public property. But I am also a family man and I love my privacy. But in Monaco it had all ended, I wasn't just another famous face and, believe me, there are plenty I was the one everybody seemed to know. I couldn't go shopping or to a restaurant with friends without being approached for my picture or my autograph. And paparazzi seemed to be everywhere.'

He used to rent a £1,000-a-week apartment in Monte Carlo and his £250,000 twin-engined high-speed cruiser was berthed in Monaco's harbour. To reach his ten-seater jet parked at Nice Airport he would either take a short helicopter journey, drive there in his £500,000 Bugatti or his Ferrari bought at a discount and not free from the factory or take his Harley-Davidson motorcycle. Despite possessing all these toys he believes that he is sensible with his earnings, 'I am earning an amount of money that others can only dream about but I don't squander and waste it,' he says. 'Sure, I drive nice cars and have my own aeroplane. I get to countries that friends I had at school and afterwards into my teens will never see, places they can only imagine. I could be somebody's paid guest somewhere different in the world every day of the week. It's crazy. But I just do not have the time to take up all the offers whatever money they offer.'

Fame and success have altered Schumacher's life for good. He says, 'I am afraid I grew away from all my schoolfriends in my little home town near Cologne but I have had to get used to being without them. I live out of Germany and it is impossible for me to stay in contact with all the kids I grew up with. That is not to say I don't ever think of them or wonder how they are. But my whole life has changed dramatically, it is hardly my own, and I am, for most of the time, somebody else's property. The demands, not just from racing and testing, are enormous. I love my home and my family life, my wife Corinna and my little daughter and our three dogs, and when I get the chance to be there I take it and I try to shut out the rest of the outside world.

Schumacher regrets the problems that have come with his success. 'Money, for sure, can buy a certain amount of privacy,' he says, 'but fame invades. I can afford now whatever I want and I have worked hard to get to that position but if the pleasures are intruded upon then the advantages of money and fame become distinct disadvantages. They count for nothing. I have to set up a wall around myself these days when I am away from home, and my manager and press officer and the team at Ferrari when we are at the track racing or testing, all help. If I didn't block people out, I would get no peace at all.'

Schumacher is often concerned with people's perception of his personality and he fears that by blocking people out he will make himself unpopular. He says, 'I know this could well be regarded as arrogance or big-headedness, but I would hate that to be the feeling people have of me because it would not be an accurate picture, far from it. And it would be wrong to suggest that it does not hurt me when people who know no better or who do not know anything about me call me arrogant or conceited. I certainly do not feel or intend to be arrogant or cold or distant. I like the practical jokes played around the team maybe not quite so cruel as the ones Gerhard Berger used to play but I enjoy having a laugh. That is my nature, even if I do look serious to outsiders. In fact, I myself do not like arrogance.

'I hate it when I meet people I consider are arrogant and offhand. I can't handle it and I would hate to work with anybody who was like that. But I am sensible enough to realize that you cannot expect everybody to like you. Some drivers like each other, some hate the sight of one another. It's nature and you can only hope that people like you for what you are as a person or admire you for what you do in your job. You can't force them.'

Schumacher frequently worries about what other people

think of him. On another occasion he said, 'I wish more people knew me. I want them to know me as I really am. But that cannot be, because of my situation. I am isolated. Even so, we all like to be liked. It is human nature.'

It is perhaps because he does not feel that his public persona reflects his private character that Schumacher cares what others think of him. There are many facets to Schumacher's personality that are far removed from the popular opinion of him as a stiff, rather uneasy character. For example, he keeps a stray dog a flea-bitten mongrel picked off the streets of Sao Paulo, showered and shampooed and transported from Brazil to Europe in his private plane. He and Corinna live a simple life away from the racetrack, their tight circle of friends are from outside the hurly-burly of celebrity wannabe friends, unlike some other champion drivers who collect hangers-on as velcro attracts fluff. 'I much prefer it that way,' says Schumacher. 'I don't like the wild life and discos I have never been interested in one-night stands. I am much happier having a nice quiet dinner, either at home or in restaurant, with a few good friends.'

If Schumacher knows how to relax at home there are signs that, to some extent, he is now able to relax during races because he has now proved himself as one of the best. He says, 'There are drivers who have never won a race or even been on the podium, never mind won a championship, and I believe there is far more pressure on them to win than there is, in my mind, on me to do it again.' But he adds, 'Whatever else I achieve I don't yet feel over the moon because there is still much more I want to do. It has always been the same for me, right from being a kid and racing karts; I come back to earth very quickly. I keep my feet firmly fixed on the ground once I am down again from whatever heights I have just been. But if there is something that fills me with great pride and personal satisfaction it is being Germany's first Formula One world champion.'

Damon Hill

Like Schumacher Damon Hill is another homebird. He spends as much time as possible with his wife Georgie and their children at their home in Dublin. Indeed, he has now acquired a jet to get him back to Ireland from races as quickly as possible. Damon's joy after the breakthrough victory for Jordan, Hill's twenty-second race win in the Belgium Grand Prix, was unbridled but still he couldn't wait to see his four children.

Hill's success at the Spa-Francorchamps circuit must have seemed light years away when he was working as a motorbike courier. As a newly-wed with a young family to support, he funded his racing through his despatch rider earnings in London while living in a crumbling Victorian terraced house in the downbeat and unfashionable Bucharest Road in Wandsworth. There were not many pleasures for Damon at that time but there were plenty of privations.

His famous father Graham, twice the Formula One world champion, perished when a light aircraft he was piloting back from a test in winter 1975 to his impressive thirty-two-room

mansion in thirty acres of grounds in the Hertfordshire countryside crashed in flames at Elstree. The accident left the family in
dire financial circumstances as the plane was uninsured and all
five passengers died. The outcome of the legal wranglings
burdened Graham's widow Bette with crippling financial settlements, making life far from easy for Damon and his sisters,
Samantha and Bridget.

The crash was also devastating emotionally for Damon. He
had just started to get close to a father who had just announced
his retirement and so was able to see more of his family. Just
three months before the fatal plane crash they had been on holiday to St Tropez together, trail-riding motorbikes in the Riviera
hills, and Graham had confided how proud he was of his only
son.

'At last I felt that we were starting to do more together,'
recalls Damon. 'I was really sold on bikes, they were a fixation,
my heroes were Barry Sheene, Freddie Spencer and Kenny
Roberts and we were having a terrific time. My dad watched me
handling the bike and told me how proud he was. He could see
I could manage the machine OK and I was at home on it. It was
very meaningful for me to know that I had impressed him. I
can't explain how devastating his death was to me. I had no idea
what to do next. But I learned a lesson, too. You have just got to
get on with your life.'

Heartache and frustration dogged Hill's formative years. 'I
was remote from my father,' he says. 'I used to be able to hear
him in his study, which was directly under my bedroom, talking
on the telephone to famous people and to all parts of the world.
And I was never part of it. I would go inside just to sit and listen

to him speaking on the phone. But I never got the chance to actually talk to him. I didn't have his attention. I didn't have him, really. We were never that close. But I knew he was famous. Maybe that was the problem.'

Damon was two years old when his father, a late Formula One starter, became world champion at the age of thirty-three. From then on Graham's life was on a crazy spiral that propelled him into the nation's affection. He was a handsome daredevil, a former Henley oarsman married to an Elizabeth Taylor lookalike who had found her own fame as a European rowing champion, and his exploits, such as taking his trousers off and dancing on a table at The Dorchester, only endeared him to his adoring fans. The gulf that grew between Damon and his increasingly famous father was an inevitable by-product of the celebrity that can cruelly breach and strain family relationships.

Damon wasn't always interested in racing but he liked going to the track because it gave him a chance to see his father. 'I can't remember anybody ever saying to me, "Would you like to go out to a circuit and see your dad driving?"' he says. 'Nobody asked. Nobody said it. It was just assumed that I was going to love cars because I was Graham Hill's son. I went to races because I didn't have any choice, not because they held any appeal for me. I couldn't even see the cars going past. It was just a load of noise to me. But if there was the slightest chance I could spend time with him I loved it. I loved being in his company, even if it meant following him around for hours.

'He enjoyed shooting he was such a good all-round sports-man and he would usually let me tag along and load for him. It wasn't much, but it gave me the chance to see the extraordinary effect he could have on people.'

While the public was enthralled by Graham, his children felt a little bit neglected by their father. 'Everybody loved him, he was such a natural show-off,' says Damon. 'And when you were a racing driver in those days you could do what the hell you liked. The neighbours near our house in Mill Hill in north London were always complaining about the wild parties that raved on all night in marquees set up on the lawn. When the police arrived they usually joined in. It was a fantasy life and my sisters and I were always packed off to bed. And when mum and dad were away racing and travelling, as they were so often, we were looked after by a string of au-pair girls. It was OK, but it is not the same as having your parents around.

'I made up my mind when I got married and became a dad that I was going to stay as close as possible to my kids whatever happened. And being away from them racing is my only sadness about the sport. I hate not having them around. If every grand prix could be run in my back garden and I could be home with them ten minutes after the finish of a race I would be one happy man. The harsh fact is that racing does take a toll of your home life and on your spirit. You have to have enormous self-discipline to stick through it and get the compromise right.'

Despite his difficult start in life Hill rocketed from poverty to a position as a modestly paid test driver before achieving multi-millionaire status at Williams collecting a world title and twenty-two GP wins along the way. He says, 'It is not so long ago that I have forgotten that I was dead broke. I didn't have two pennies to rub together. I had no job, no prospects, a mortgage, and we had just had our first child, Oliver, who was a Downs Syndrome baby. It was pretty bleak. And, yeah, I had to fend for myself, but I don't want it to sound as if I had it really tough. Certainly, it wasn't as tough for us as it was for a lot of other people. But it was hard enough for it to be uncomfortable at times.'

In those days he would press his home telephone number and address, printed on a rather skimpily presented, cheap and austere business card, into anybody's hands if he thought they could help him. Having come such a long way the normally modest Damon is proud of his achievements. 'It has all been due to my own efforts. I didn't get anything because I had a nice smile or because I was Graham Hill's son. It is because I could use these to good effect,' he said, spreading his hands and tapping his heart and his head.

A family man and a racing man, Damon fiercely disagrees with racing tyrant Enzo Ferrari's sneering assertion that a driver with dependants penalizes himself at least one second a lap because subconsciously he is backing away from the risk that he should be taking to win. 'Not at all,' says Damon, 'I fight for my family. And I race as hard as I can and, cruel and callous as it may seem, I don't even think about them or consider them when I am out there doing my stuff. I can't afford to allow any distractions or split-second doubts and hesitations about whether I should go for it and overtake or not because I've got a young family. I have to keep my concentration at a maximum to stop me falling off the road. My wife and my children are my life at home. Not on the track. That is where my job is. That is my office. It is where I earn my living and their security for the future. Afterwards, when it is all over and done with win or lose, champion or not, bad race or good I just enjoy cuddling them and getting down to the joy of being a dad. They don't care whether I'm famous or the champion, but they do love to see the champagne spray on the podium. They think it's hilarious to seen grown men splashing each other. That's real mad fun to them.

'The moments when I am home doing the normal dad things like taking them to school or going for walks in the lovely Irish countryside with them put it all in perspective for me. It is why I can cope with the danger, the insecurity that can worry you, and it is the reason why I stick my neck out. I can promise you there is no feeling that beats their little arms around my neck no silverware, how ever impressive or important, can match that extra-special sensation. I could be accused of having my cake and eating it because I want to race and have a family. But I feel that my father was an example to me, and he was the person he was for what he did. And this is a challenge which gives me as much meaning to my life as having a family.'

Despite his rebuttal of Ferrari's dictum Hill admits that when Senna, his Williams teammate at the time, was killed, he had deep discussions with his wife about carrying on. He says, 'When Ayrton was killed we talked it over, but we came to the same conclusion together that it would be unrealistic for me to quit because I would not be happy unless I was racing. It is not easy when you see somebody crash to their death. It all makes you realize just how fragile a human being is. In 1994, in Portugal, I tipped my car over at fifty miles an hour. If I had landed on the barrier I wouldn't have needed any speed at all.

The car would have broken my neck. When you drive a car at the speeds we do you are exposing yourself to a lot of risk and a times you do need a bit of luck.

'There are a lot of risks involved, but the job is more challenging because of them and I came to terms with that a long time ago. But I don't want to be a sorry story and I certainly would not want a son of mine to be a racer. I couldn't bear the thought of them hurting themselves, or worse. Anyway, I think there are far more rewarding things to do and I wouldn't want to see them exposed to the risk.'

Despite, or perhaps because of, the risks they take, Formula One drivers are often a cosseted bunch. At one stage, when Damon was at Williams and his fame and achievements were at their peak, he had a meddlesome mother hen of a press officer who used to draw imaginary demarcation lines on the ground to indicate the limit beyond which jostling media questioners were forbidden to cross at interviews behind Hill's pit lane garage.

The paranoia among the Formula One teams showed itself yet again when a Sunday tabloid published a photograph of the front door of his new home in Dublin. Even though the picture showed a door indistinguishable from a million other houses in Ireland, Hill was furious. Bumping into him at Nice Airport I was on the receiving end of a remarkably naive tirade. Another time, in the lead up to the British Grand Prix at Silverstone, Damon's boss at Arrows, Tom Walkinshaw, gave me an exclusive interview in which he said that he felt that Damon was not performing as a world champion should, particularly for the money he was being paid, and that he was making the car look far worse than it really was. Walkinshaw, typically forthright, added that Damon's job was on the line, saying, 'If he doesn't pull his finger out there are plenty of other drivers out there who would be happy to do the job.' The message was clear and it had serious implications for a man who was being paid £4.5 million to drive the car. As a device to spur Damon on, it was a clever one.

The newspapers which had been scooped wound an angry Hill up into believing that Walkinshaw had never said it, and despite the interview being on my tape the Arrows owner denied he had made those comments. (He later apologised.) Hill went into a towering rage, and I was the target. It came to a head when he lost control and I was physically manhandled out of the Arrows hospitality unit in front of an astonished group of onlookers. Someone had pricked the bubble that protects the drivers and Hill didn't like it.

No doubt partly as a result of Walkinshaw's reported comments Damon's driving showed an immediate improvement and he finished sixth in the race. 'Well, that worked OK,' Walkinshaw said to me, later in the paddock, with a wicked wink. Formula One people will, it seems, use any device or anybody or anything to achieve their aims.

Although Hill can appear to be a gentle soul he has been known to lose his temper on other occasions. When he partnered Alain Prost at Williams the French legend counselled Damon to curb his rages in the garage. Some time later Hill believed that controlling his temper had helped him to become a better driver. He said, 'To be world champion you have to want it a lot and you have to be disciplined. It is always slightly painful to have people point out where you have got it wrong, but there is nobody more aware of those things than myself. Conversely, I know where I got it right. It is all about being honest with yourself, committing yourself in the areas you feel could have been better. I think one of my strengths is that I learn and I adapt. I can always improve if I need to. It is one of the most challenging aspects of the sport and it is what makes it so satisfying. You are given a set of challenges and you try to conquer them by learning and improving in both your physical preparation and your mental approach.

Prost's comments helped Damon to realize that he didn't have to fight the world as there were people on his side. 'I learned to trust other people,' he said. 'I feel now that people are there to help me and I don't push them away and say "No, I want to do it myself." I actually use people around me to make my life easier so that I can focus on my driving.

'I have confidence in myself, to be honest. I feel an intense need to prove myself to myself and it used to be that I didn't want to be helped. I didn't want it suggested that any sort of achievement had been the result of some sort of handicap system. Maybe that comes from being the son of somebody famous, of always being seen as privileged, so I was always anti-help. I have always wanted to achieve things for myself without help but I don't feel that any more. I feel I can draw on all the people around me and it has lifted a great burden off me. But it is an essential part of my make-up to push myself, not with any big need to try and impress others. I like to believe that if I do well, everybody can enjoy a good performance and get some satisfaction from seeing somebody performing to their very best. For me it is crucial to know that I could not have done any better.'

Hill could not have done any better in 1996 than win the world championship and he was disappointed that there were some who wrote off his successes at Williams as being due to the car rather than the driver. 'It blighted my life there,' he says, 'and there was continual insinuation that another driver could have done a better job than I did. But it just does not stack up. After all, I did win the title. A championship is not handed to you like a gift, you have to fight for it and I won more races than my teammates. Sure I was in a good-class car, the best, but I had to have the talent to make use of it.'

That philosophy is difficult to dispute, but it is easy not to sympathize with him in his plight as yet another Frank Williams cast-off. He had always argued that a driver can recognize his value to a team by what they are prepared to pay him. How that ethic squared with his rejection of a contract with McLaren-Mercedes for 1998 when they were prepared to pay him a £1.5 million retainer and win bonuses of £600,000 capped at four and graduated thereafter, is not easy to understand.

Damon ended up joining TWR Arrows after his mysterious sacking by Frank Williams at the end of his championship year. He had been deluged with accolades, prizes, win bonuses, silverware from around the globe, an OBE and had been voted BBC Television Personality of the Year. But there was no likelihood that he would win the championship the following year. He joked, 'If I get an award at the end of this season it will be for best supporting performer.' He was, he claimed, as puzzled as any punter about his dismissal by Williams. But it is thought that it was because he asked for more money than Frank Williams, a notoriously tough negotiator, was prepared to pay. The rumour has a certain amount of credibility as the previous year Bernie Ecclestone had negotiated on Hill's behalf and secured a deal for him which might at the time, when he hadn't yet won a championship, have been more than he was worth. Ecclestone felt that Damon should have taken the new Williams offer as he would have been driving a car that was odds-on to win the title the following year. It did, but with Jacques Villeneuve behind the wheel.

Damon was unhappy about the outcome of the negotiations, saying, 'I don't believe what happened was right, in that I won the championship. I worked hard with Williams and I felt I deserved the right to defend my title in that car. But that is not the way of Formula One and there are other factors.' What the 'other factors' were remained Damon's secret.

In his second full season at Williams, when he had already registered five wins from only twenty-eight starts Damon had unwittingly foreseen the future. He said: 'It is always wrong to feel established. There are no permanent fixtures in Formula One, although I suppose if you win a world championship you are a little better off.' Little did he realize how wrong he would later be shown to be.

There can be no doubt that Hill's resilience has been severely tested over the years both on and off the track and, despite his record and his victory strike rate, he has many doubters. But he argues, 'The only way to rate a driver is to look at his results. And how do you rate my record? I think it is pretty good.' Before his switch to Arrows, where only hydraulics failure prevented him from winning the 1997 Hungarian Grand Prix, and his marvellous victory for Jordan in Belgium a year later, which gave him a remarkable record of having led a grand prix in every season in which he had competed, he had established himself as one of the all-time top points scorers, on a par with any of the great champions. Damon believes that the reason he has been able to accumulate so many points is not just the car or his driving skills. 'If I had to sum up my strength in one word it would be my determination,' he says. 'For as long as I can remember I have always wanted to do better than I have done before.'

Interestingly, when asked to consider who he thinks will make a future champion Damon is quick to suggest a fellow Briton. He says, 'When I look at other drivers as possible future champions I see David Coulthard. You can't take anything away from him. He has shown he is a world-class driver with the potential to be world champion.'

David Coulthard

D avid Coulthard's qualities extend far beyond those of being an accomplished driver in the top bracket. To know him is to like him, not only for his natural friendliness, his manners, his sense of humour and boyish enthusiasm for racing, but for his highly developed sense of integrity. He is the last of the Corinthian spirits in Formula One. That is why it was so sad to see him reviled by Michael Schumacher after their collision at the 1998 Belgian Grand Prix. 'Are you trying to fucking kill me?' yelled the German as he was forcibly pulled back from his attack. 'He was like an animal,' commented a shocked Coulthard, before adding with typical understatement and aplomb, 'That is totally unacceptable behaviour.' He then proffered an invitation, 'If Schumacher wants to sit down and talk man to man so we can discuss it on our own then I have no problem with that. But if he is accusing me then I have no interest in talking to him. It was disgusting behaviour for someone who has such a fantastic record. He needs to get help to control his temper.'

In the event they met on neutral ground, the Williams motorhome at the Italian Grand Prix in Monza, and were photographed shaking hands.

While the stewards listened to Ferrari's official protest they absolved Coulthard from any blame. But in the immediate aftermath and despite the explanations and the telemetric evidence Schumacher, so often the perpetrator but now the furious victim with little or no sympathy from any quarter but his own team, refused to apologize. Instead, Schumacher, forever looking for justification, fumed, 'We believe there is something more behind this ... I was fighting for the championship. We should have left Spa with a three-point lead in the championship. Instead we left seven points behind. And, yes, it is true I asked him if he wanted to kill me. Lifting off on the straight as he did doesn't help anyone in these kind of conditions. I don't believe it was the right way to behave.'

His technical director Ross Brawn then added fuel to the fire by saying, 'This was simply not a professional move by a racing driver and I assume that is what David Coulthard thinks he is. The consequences could have been more serious.'

In the heat of the row it was worth recalling the words of Niki Lauda who described Coulthard as 'easily the most complete performer. He is friendly, controlled and calm. He is one hell of a driver and is completely fair.'

Of course, the idea that any driver would willingly risk his own life by suddenly and maliciously lifting off the throttle or jabbing the brake in front of a car being driven by a man as hell-bent on winning as Schumacher was – he was driving at 150-or-so miles an hour in almost zero visibility on a rain-drenched track – would render him automatically certifiable. It is unlikely that someone who had to make the sacrifices that the young Scot did to reach the top flight would do anything so dangerous.

It was his father Duncan, a reasonably well-off haulage contractor in the Scottish borders village of Twynholm, who push-started the young Coulthard. 'I bought David a go-kart for a Christmas present when he was twelve,' says Duncan. 'And without telling him I entered him for a race three days later. It was a pretty hectic and dramatic start to his race career he turned it upside down on the very first corner. But, typically, it didn't put him off and he was hooked. He took to it like a natural. He was Scottish junior champion in 1983, 1984 and 1985. And the Scottish Open and British Super One kart champion in 1986 and 1987. And then in 1988, when he was sixteen, he was the Scottish Open kart champion again.

'When he went onto single-seater car racing in 1989 he won his first race at Thruxton in a Formula Ford 1600. It was quite amazing. It was wet and conditions generally were terrible. Everything was against a newcomer taking his first victory but he was wonderfully smooth and he won the race by miles.'

But while all his pals around his village home were discovering their youth in the way growing boys do David was missing out. However, he doesn't regret that he was so focused on cars in his youth. He explains, 'I have made all the sacrifices to get this far in my career and I can honestly say I do not regret anything I may have missed.

'OK, all my mates were finding out about girls and having a good time at parties and discos and I was rushing to circuits up and down the country, day and night, trying to be a racing driver. I wasn't interested in booze and girls, I was too determined to justify my mum and dad's faith in me and be a success in racing cars. I like to think I am what I am because of my upbringing. My father was always my driving force while my mother was the relaxing influence. They were crucial to me.

'I do not think I missed anything and I certainly don't mope about what might have been even though for four years of my mid-teens I had something to do – either working on my car or racing it – every single night of the week. I knew my mates were living it up somewhere and I was up to my elbows in grease. I must have seemed to be the most boring boy in the world, but it is what I wanted to do, it was my own choice, and having what was reckoned to be a good time with a few beers and late nights out at parties or pubs was very much in the background and at the lowest end of my priorities so far as I was concerned.

'I gave up holidays and knocking about with the lasses, and never thought twice about it, and I happily made all the sacrifices I felt were necessary because I had that target firmly fixed in my sights I was going to be a racing driver. Every lost minute of party time as a kid growing up has been worth it. Now I am exactly where I want to be short of winning the championship and I am happy and content. I couldn't be more satisfied because of what it all led to and what I have done with my life.' Besides, when he sees Heidi, the girl who shares his life among the jet-setters in Monaco, he thinks to himself, 'I have done my catching up on those lads back home.'

Coulthard was twenty-three years old when he took part in his first Formula One race, the 1994 Spanish Grand Prix. His engine started cutting out after three laps and then the throttle started to stick and there were problems with the gearbox. Although he continued for a while it was eventually decided that he should stop. His second grand prix, this time in Montreal, was more successful as he scored his first championship points with a magnificent fifth-place finish, giving his more experienced teammate, Damon Hill, a big scare. Even then Coulthard's ambition shone through as it was clear that he wanted more than to be going round in fifth place. He said of the race, 'It could have been better. I pushed a little bit hard at the start, cooked my tyres and lost the balance of the car.'

In his first British Grand Prix at Silverstone a few weeks later Coulthard again finished in fifth place despite stalling on the line and spinning at the first corner. The problems did not stop there as Coulthard also had radio problems. He recalled: 'A local taxi station despatcher broke into our frequency and he came on my radio. There was a 3.30 p.m. pick-up at Buckingham. And the guy was called David! What with the taxis coming on and off I couldn't hear the team clearly.'

Coulthard's promising start was but a sign of what was to

come. One of the most pleasing aspects of his climb up the F1 pecking order is that, unlike some of his rivals, he has been able to maintain a reputation for sportsmanship. Coulthard believes that fairness is as important as competition to sport. 'Over all the years I have been racing I have always had a sense of values and a feeling for fair play,' he says. 'I just hate cheats and dirty drivers. This business is dangerous enough without trying to push somebody off. I am not being naive, but if I can't win because I am better than the other guy and by my own honest efforts then I don't want to win. I don't know how people can live with themselves if they are cheats and that goes for any sport.

'That doesn't mean you don't have to be forceful and make your presence felt on the track. You have to be strong in that regard and show that you are not going to be the one to back off when it's all fair and square to be first into a corner.

Being responsible is a dominant theme in Coulthard's attitude to his job. 'To be any other way and not to race to your absolute maximum means you are being a let-down to the 200 or so people back at the factory who have provided the best racing car they can,' he says. 'That's a big incentive, to do your best aside from the one of natural desire to be a winner. And when I am in the car doing what I do best in life I have no doubt I do a good job. When I get out of the car after a race I think, "Jesus, this is some responsibility."

'But that's what I have groomed myself to feel: responsibility to everybody who plays a part in my career, from my dad who bought me my first kart when I was twelve and supported me when I was the junior champion of Scotland, right up to my

McLaren-Mercedes connections. I would be upset if anybody thought for one second that I wasn't giving them back as much as I could by putting in all the effort I possibly can. I may not win all the time, but it certainly isn't because I am not trying.'

It is partly because of this attitude that Coulthard is a sponsor's dream. But he does have other assets: he is tall, clean cut and handsome in the traditional heroic, square-jawed sense, and he has the ability to challenge strongly for the championship. It was his development as a driver, first testing for and then securing a race-by-race deal with Williams alongside Hill, coupled with his well-paid activities off the track, that propelled him to new-found riches which necessitated his relocation from London to the tax haven of Monte Carlo.

His Monaco lifestyle suits him though his preference for the quiet life on his rare days off usually keeps him away from the livelier bars and restaurants; when he wants some fun and company he makes for Stars and Bars, a sprawling pavement eating and drinking den on the quayside. 'I like to drop in now and again for their quiz night,' he says. 'It's brilliant fun. And you don't get pestered. The place is often packed with famous people so the customers who go there are used to a bit of celebrity. I was a main guest one night with John Collins, the Scottish footballer and Shirley Bassey was in there and sang a song. We've seen Justin Hayward from the Moody Blues at one of the quizzes and he got up and sang "Nights in White Satin". I got a cassette and he scribbled "Vroom" across it.

'I know people say it can be a boring little town, but it is nowhere near as dull and as numbing as people would like to believe. That just shows a lack of imagination. There are more things for me to do than there were in the village where I was brought up and where I spent eighteen years of my life. But you don't need to be spending thousands of pounds in the Casino to be living life as it is perceived to be for a grand prix driver. To get the motorbike out and ride with my girlfriend Heidi around the country roads and into the hills for a picnic is wonderful.'

He often goes out for meals with Jacques Villeneuve and after a session at the gym regularly bumps into Formula One's other nice guy, Johnny Herbert, at the British pub, The Ship and Castle, for teetotal evening of spa water and soft drinks. 'We are all young guys with similar lifestyles, similar outlooks and regimes,' he says. 'We are all racing drivers, but there is a normal life. I love listening to The Corrs (an Irish band) on my CD player. I share the cooking at home, though I am not very good. I fold my own laundry, I do the shopping and pay the bills.'

David Coulthard is a hugely successful young man who may well make a £50 million fortune before he quits racing, as he intends, at the age of thirty-five, in 2006. Life could not be rosier. But at one stage things, if only briefly, looked bleak. He was offloaded in another mysterious decision by Frank Williams despite a promising start in Formula One. To this day he reflects on Frank Williams's generous praise 'he is a wonderfully gifted driver, intelligent and clever' and still can't work out why he was fired. But it does not stop him being grateful to Williams for giving him a chance in the first place. Happily for Coulthard, he hardly had time to read his termination letter before McLaren stepped in and signed the man who at only nineteen years of age had been voted *Autosport* Young Driver of the Year.

Coulthard feels that he has vindicated the decision of

McLaren to take him on and is confident that he can repay their faith in him. 'I have won my place on merit and ability. That in itself is a wonderful feeling, he says, before adding, 'If I didn't think I could beat the likes of Schumacher and the others I wouldn't be in this business and if team owners didn't believe I could then they wouldn't buy my services.'

Coulthard's former girlfriend Andrea Murray, a Canadian fashion model, gave a fascinating insight into the fears and feelings of those who have to wait and watch and worry while the men they are close to go to work at 200 miles an hour. 'I get terrified watching him,' she said, 'I know exactly how many seconds each lap should take and if David's car does not reappear dead on time that split second before he does seems to last an age. It is unbearable and all the wives and girlfriends feel the same way. You just cannot explain the worry in the pit of your stomach. But the team becomes your family and your support system and they give you strength and confidence.

'I had to find a way to push the fears and the dangers to the back of my mind because I had to be seen to be supporting David. It is so hard sometimes not to show the fear and the trepidation, but I just dare not because it could undermine his confidence. It's not something I can discuss with him. I can't say to David that I am really scared.

'If I don't support him 100 per cent he will feel it. I am the closest to him. When the tension and stress get to be too much and the fears do come out, usually when we are a home, well, you just get kind of snappy with each other. It's not like he's a golfer or a tennis player or involved in some other safe sport. He is a racing driver, he has to take chances because it's his job. He

185

knows he is OK and that he can cope with just about everything that confronts him, but it is difficult for people like us who have to wait for them to come home to share that confidence.'

Andrea kept a diary when she was with David. She revealed a the time, 'It's my safety valve. My relief when the tension is building inside me. I list all the things that might go wrong. I express to myself all my worries whether there could be a blow-out or a misjudgement on a tricky section. And after the race I write how happy and relieved I am that he has come back safe and sound. Strange isn't it? Because I have such confidence in his ability and most times I am not scared. But the times I am I have to put it down in my diary. I wouldn't dream of showing it to him. It is me confiding in myself.

'Once when I got home there was a fax of a newspaper story about a crash David had. It said something like "Coulthard survives high-speed crash" and when I had read it I got very upset and angry because I had not long since spoken to him on the telephone and he had said he'd had a bit of a bump in the gravel trap. He played it all down and that really scared me. I got upset. But I had to accept that it was the way of our life and his business.

'When Senna died it was unbelievable. David thought Ayrton was immortal and that nothing could possibly happen to him. I had grown used to seeing crashes with the drivers walking away OK and unhurt and I thought that was how it always was with nobody getting hurt or killed. Trying to live with that risk that, yes, your man could die in a racing car was pretty difficult.'

Coulthard's philosophy to both risks and race strategies is quite clear. 'I don't think I take unnecessary risks,' he says. 'I work on the principle that when in doubt do nothing and know your own limits and the limits of the car, but still recognize the opportunities and take advantage of them without a split second of hesitation. At starts for instance, and I have a reputation for quick getaways, it amazes me how cautious other people can be on the first lap. A lot of people can jump in a car and be very quick, but they don't know how to be consistently fast throughout a race, and that is something I concentrate on doing. My concern has always been to make the car do its work in an easy way never forcing it to do something it doesn't want to do. There are some drivers who rely on out-and-out speed which might be OK for maybe five laps but then they find they have gone over the limit and are doing five slow laps.'

While he is generally held to be one of the quickest drivers Coulthard also has a reputation as one of the calmest drivers in F1. 'I certainly feel very relaxed in the car, I don't get like that because I spend half an hour before a race in a darkened room listening to whale sounds,' he says. 'I don't need to use any tricks to be calm it is the way I am by nature. And when I start up the engine for the warm-up lap of a grand prix it is the most fantastic and exciting feeling I know. That's when I know it is down to me and as soon as I get out there on the track all the pressure that has built up evaporates.'

His famous cool and considered unflustered reactions in the most stressful of situations were never more evident that when he crashed quite heavily when he was running third in Hungary during only his fifth grand prix. Frank Williams saw the race on the television monitors in the pit lane garage and he recalled, 'I saw him spin and even before he hit the barrier he was on the radio as cool as a cucumber saying "I've lost it, I'm going to crash. I don't know what happened. When the car stops I'll get out, walk back and re-run the accident in my mind and work out what happened."'

Four years after his Formula One debut Coulthard's calmness has helped him to become one of the highest-rated drivers in the sport. His boss at McLaren, Ron Dennis, thinks of him as a champion of the future and this view is enthusiastically endorsed by Mercedes racing chief Norbert Haug who raucously celebrates every Coulthard victory by playing 'Davy's on the Road Again' at full volume on the ghetto blaster in the McLaren-Mercedes hospitality unit. For the moment, however, it is Mika Hakkinen who leads the McLaren challenge. Coulthard understands why he has played second fiddle to Hakkinen in the 1998 season but he doesn't expect that situation to remain unchanged. He says, 'I feel very much part of the team, but I will never get over the fact that Mika has been with them longer than I have and has been very much supported by Ron. The emotional bond between them is stronger because they have been through a lot together. Until I consistently out-race and out-qualify Mika it will always be the same. In that respect, the ball is in my court.'

But it is not just the people within the McLaren-Mercedes team who believe that Coulthard can become world champion. Even rival team owner Jackie Stewart is confident that he has the ability to take on and beat the rest. 'Above everything else, he is a good racer,' says the three-time world champion. 'Sometimes you get good drivers, sometimes you get guys with plenty of natural talent and a good level of intelligence but unless they are genuine racers those other assets won't be enough in the final analysis. There are people who can drive very well but do not have the spark which, for example, in the first three laps of a race, will enable them to carve their way through the traffic towards the front. Great natural talent does not always have that positive edge but David has it aplenty. It will make him a champion.'

BERNIE ECCLESTONE

**Chief Executive of Formula One
Administration Ltd,
Vice President of FIA in charge
of Promotional Affairs**

lthough he stands at barely 5 ft 4 in Bernie Ecclestone's gaunt face, darkened spectacles and tumble of unfashionably long grey hair somehow contrive to cut a menacing appearance. He is one of the most intriguing figures of his generation, an awesome man of power and mystery yet his handshake is a fleeting, brushing one. 'What is he really like?' is perhaps the Formula One question I am most frequently asked.

'Good friend ... bad enemy,' was his own laughing response when I put the question to him at his nine-storey Knightsbridge offices, a building he bought from Middle East arms merchant Adnan Khashoggi for £7 million. His office suite is situated on the ground floor although he prefers to do most of his interview and conference business in the austere waiting room, with visitors seated around a table while he opts disarmingly to stand or lean against the window ledge. In the waiting room there is a mock stack of $4 million dollars piled up on a plinth. You can't help but think that even if it were real and not plastic it would be small change to one of Britain's wealthiest men. Ecclestone paid himself £29.7 million in 1994, £29.4 million in 1995 and £54 million in 1997. In 1996 he took Britain's biggest-ever wage cut, paying himself only £600,000, in order to divert funds into his adventurous television operation.

It both puzzles and amuses him that the level of deference shown to him by internationally influential power brokers, politicians and celebrities, borders on the subservient at times. He protests that he is 'just a guy doing a job to the best of his ability'. That's like a brain surgeon writing his own job description as somebody who clips fingernails for a living.

Ecclestone's undoubted and remarkable entrepreneurial ability has lifted grand prix racing from a weekend pastime where the idle rich got together for a jolly good thrash around a race circuit to a worldwide business worth countless millions of pounds.

Grand prix grandees, too busy being Corinthian to trouble themselves about hard commerce for the sport's greater benefit, were only too happy to hand over control of commercial development to a businessman of Ecclestone's impeccable credentials. Exactly why and how he persuaded them that he was the man for them is something Ecclestone, who enjoys intrigue, is in no hurry to throw light on. One thing is clear, however: the day they granted him the rights to do the job was a lucky day for grand prix racing.

It seems as though those in charge sat back and listened when he outlined his plan for Formula One. Lord Hesketh, James Hunt's mentor and President of the British Racing Drivers' Club (BDRC), recalled that, 'When Bernie said "this is the way it should be done" everybody said "OK, Bernie, get on with it."'

Bernie's antecedents were impressive. In 1971 he formed Motor Racing Developments (MRD), in order to manufacture motor racing cars and participate in worldwide motor racing events. Its subsidiary, International Race Tyres Limited, supplied and dealt in motor race tyres. In 1975 MRD turned over £300,000 but inside eight years that figure had leapt to £6 million. Business was booming and Ecclestone's stock as an entrepreneur was sky high. The self-confessed wheeler-dealer, who as an eleven year old had bought and sold fountain pens and bicycles and anything else he felt he could trade at school, was perfect for the role of architect of motor racing's expansion.

In the late 1970s he later formed the Formula One Constructors' Association (FOCA) and in the late 1980s, after a few skirmishes with the FIA hierarchy, convinced the teams that if they were united as a force they could maximize their earning power. The teams did not need much persuading once Ecclestone had outlined the possibilities of burgeoning global sponsorship and television markets in return for an attractive package of inter-national personalities, larger-than-life drivers and moving advertising placards called Formula One cars. In 1997 Formula One was reckoned by an international business assessor to have a turnover of around £130 million, boosted by a tenfold increase in TV revenue after ITV took over screening the sport from the BBC in a £70 million seven-year deal. Income in 1997 more than trebled the 1994 figure of £37 million.

Ecclestone is modest about his role in Formula One's commercial growth, saying, 'It was obvious. It needed to be done. I could see the openings and the possibilities. They just needed to be exploited properly. I am good for the FIA. They know me, they know they can trust me. They realize their busi-ness is in good hands and they know I generate most of the money for the FIA.'

However, Max Mosley, the FIA President and a long-term

ally, is happy to sing Ecclestone's praises, saying, 'Bernie has made himself a very wealthy man, but he had to take some bloody big risks to do it. He deserves every penny he has got he has certainly earned them. He has made fortunes for a lot of other people and has worked wonders for Formula One. Nobody else but he could have done it. He is a genius and we should all be grateful.'

It is not hard to find people who are prepared to compliment Ecclestone on his business acumen. Carlos Reutemann, once a driver and now a high-flying politician in his native Argentina, says, 'Bernie puts the same effort into working for one dollar as he does for a milllion.' Niki Lauda, the 1975, 1977 and 1984 champion once managed by Ecclestone, says, 'He is quite the coruscating character everybody believes him to be and completely unpredictable into the bargain. When you find yourself negotiating with him you have to be on top form because he will use any excuse. And he twists and turns to such a degree there is no thread to his conversation that you can grasp.' Mosley adds, 'He is technically an excellent negotiator, and he can extract a higher percentage from what is available in a deal than anybody I know.'

Ecclestone brushes aside the compliments in the manner of a man who has had more than his fair share of them. He claims that his attitude is to 'be fair with people but strict, too.' He explains, 'If you let some people do what they want in this game God only knows what might happen. Of course, from time to time there is dissension in the ranks with such a varied bunch of people it's only to be expected and the big problem is that we have all grown up together. When there is no money involved, the family's united. But change it around, bring money in, and the family starts to think it should have a bit more.

'Over the years I have tried my best to help struggling teams but it's like there is somebody drowning. You chuck them a lifebelt and when they make it to safety on the shore they complain that you are a bloody idiot, that you hit them on the head with the lifebelt. You can't win.'

Bernie prefers not to give too much away, either because of the demands on his time or because of his own inclination to stay out of the limelight as much as is practicable in such a high-profile position. He says without a trace of a smile, 'There are two things I don't talk about . . . last night and my money.'

Ecclestone has a rascal's sense of humour. On one occasion, during the Portuguese Grand Prix, he instructed a Fleet Street notable to invite his tabloid colleagues to a dinner party in a splendid beachside fish restaurant outside Estoril. Come midnight at the party, which everybody agreed had been a riot of fun and jokes and storytelling in true Fleet Street fashion, Bernie returned to his hotel but insisted generously, 'I have to go, but don't let me spoil the party. You guys stay on, have a good time.'

With that the benefactor was gone in his chauffeur-driven limousine. Fleet Street's finest, warming to Bernie's munificence and extolling the virtues of their now absent friend let the champagne and brandies flow and raided the humidor. The party only halted when it was evident the waiters wanted to go home.

Out trooped a merry band of appreciative hacks ... only to be stopped at the door by the restaurant manager proffering a sizeable bill for the drinks and cigars that had been ordered after Ecclestone had settled his account for the dinner. It was Bernie at his wicked best.

A wartime trawlerman's son from St Peter's, a village in Suffolk, Ecclestone is, he insists, working class. His voice and his accent betray nothing of his roots. The delivery is pitched in a low tone and the sentences, in the manner of a man who thinks he should already be elsewhere, are staccato and economically brief. As Chief Executive of Formula One Administration, Vice-President of FIA and the head of a fast-expanding TV empire, started with £60 million of his own money, with digital fingers reaching into countries desperate for development of the medium, Ecclestone is now right at the heart of Formula One. He is sixty-eight, but his energy, his quickness of mind, his stickler's eye for detail that runs even to the precise parking-up in registration-plate order of his fleet of television trucks at the track, and his ruthlessness in business, despite what would normally be considered a risky trust in a handshake on deals worth upwards of £3 million, is without bounds. So are his opinions. With a crooked smile and an unguarded, barbed comment Ecclestone will cut right to the heart of Formula One matter.

I suggest he is regarded as the runner of a world show, a ring-master, a power broker ... Formula One's supremo. He interrupts: 'To be frank I don't give a fuck what people call me, the titles give me neither pleasure or displeasure, and as far as being featured in your book – well, sport, I'm not interesting enough.'

Despite his protestations, it is mind-boggling to imagine the multi-million-pound stratospheric deals that must have been conducted and completed across his Knightsbridge desk; the internationally famous celebrities and influential business and political notables who have come into play in the great grand prix game under Ecclestone's steerage would fill a *Who's Who*. Yet he is never boastful about their friendship nor impressed by their importance, and will treat the most famous film star in the world, the greatest driver, financier, politician or billionaire sponsor, the same way as he would you or me.

Part of the fascination of Ecclestone is his mystique, a deliberately developed and carefully sustained aura pierced by only a handful of trusted friends and associates.

An appearance from behind the blacked-out windows of his trackside silver grey bus HQ, known as the Kremlin, for the briefest walk through the throng in the paddock at a race, dressed in his customary dark trousers, white shirt and loafers, stirs a swarm of interested parties. The bystanders may want a nod of recognition, sanction on the run on a deal that could be worth millions, or just to be seen by envious onlookers to be receiving the Ecclestone equivalent of a papal blessing.

He dispenses greetings and bonhomie on the move and rarely breaks stride, except from time to time to dart into a hospitality unit to say hello to somebody he has spotted. It might be Placido Domingo, Boris Becker, the Duchess of York, Ronaldo, King Juan Carlos of Spain, Prince Albert of Monaco, Phil Collins, Paul Newman, or any one of the 500 or so VIP guests who apply for paddock passes at each race and who are personally vetted and accredited or denied access by Ecclestone himself.

Sometimes his frankness about people is startling. He is particularly harsh on those who veer without direction or absolute control of their destiny and those who upset him by their ineptitude or incompetence. When interviewing him, the unspoken message is that you don't ask and, anyway, he won't tell you unless he feels the greater good of Formula One is served or he wants to get something off his chest and he knows you won't embarrass him by trumpeting what he has told you. Then, short of confidences being betrayed, anything goes.

A high-profile driver who, in Ecclestone's opinion, had suddenly begun to value himself ridiculously highly, had a manager whose blatant disregard for restraint, common sense and Bernie's advice recklessly blew a deal for a drive in one of the leading teams. Ecclestone felt that it would have been an ideal placement, but a clumsy negotiating move with a notoriously immovable and ruthless team owner effectively ended whatever chance the driver had of matching his towering skill with a winning car. Afterwards Bernie told me, 'You know so-and-so don't you? What does he call himself? A contracts negotiator! He couldn't bloody well negotiate his way from my desk to the exit and it's a straight line. The money he wanted was ridiculous. I told him the driver was good, but not that good. And if Ayrton Senna was reincarnated at the peak of his form he could have expected to be paid that sort of money, but his man was certainly no Senna.' He revealed both men's identities, knowing full well he could trust me not to pass them on, because he wanted to demonstrate the difficulties he faces but cannot always control when somebody spurns his advice.

Money, and vast amounts of it, may be central to the Formula One business but you get the distinct impression from Ecclestone that he simply views his income as a yardstick. He says, 'People do get rewarded for their performance and their ability if it is good enough, no matter who they are or what they do. I don't feel I am any different. I am probably not worth any of the money I am supposed to get. But, really, money in large amounts is just one way of keeping score of your efforts and successes. It is a reward in a way for all the work I do. And I do a lot.' He adds, 'But I enjoy it and I suppose, even though I keep threatening to retire, I will drop dead doing this job, probably sitting at this desk.'

Ecclestone attributes some of his success to the hardships of his childhood. 'When I grew up in the countryside, long before my dad changed his job and became an engineer and we moved to Dartford in Kent, we lived in a tiny house with an outside toilet,' he says. 'We had to takes baths in a tin tub in the kitchen and water for it had to be boiled on top of the stove.'

He views his childhood with a mixture of disbelief at the memory of the hardship and affection for how his close-knit family mother, father and sister retained a high sense of values despite their poor circumstances. 'The years when people tend to get a character or grow up is between, I suppose, when they are nine or so years old and into their teens. At the time of the war I was nine so I grew up knowing all about shortages and want and the need to have values. And it wasn't easy. Nothing was easy. I had to fight all the way.'

Ecclestone grew in everything but stature and it was quickly apparent that he had a formidable talent for business. 'I left school early because I wanted to, before I was fifteen,' he says. 'The old man didn't want me to pack up, he just wanted me to have a better chance in life than he'd had, to be better than they were. So we struck a deal. And it was that if he let me leave I had to go and continue in a job connected with what I was studying: physics and chemistry. I joined the Gas Company in Dartford and went to work in their laboratory. But it was mundane work, just checking bottles of stuff and seeing that everything was OK in the lab, and it kept me hanging on to my sense of values and working out for myself that there was something better to be had if I was prepared to put in some effort and take a chance or two.

'It also woke me up to the idea there was a bit of trade to be done in transport motorbikes. I recognized a gap in the market and a good chance to make a few quid. And I used to buy and sell them on the Gas Works number. I started my business life wheeling and dealing from the lab. The phone was always ringing for me.'

The Gas Company did not realize it, but they were responsible for initially funding and enabling a bored but precociously entrepreneurial embryonic businessman to put himself on the path to a personal fortune estimated in 1998 at £250 million. Now the controller of a Formula One enterprise worth £1.5 billion, at the Gas Company he was a £15 a week lab assistant.

The trade in motorbikes, in a post-war era where there was petrol rationing and a desperate shortage of suitable and viable transport, was a godsend for an ambitious and enterprising young man provided he had the wit and the wherewithal to function in a notoriously tough trade. 'I am still wheeling and dealing these days so nothing has changed only the business I am in,' says Ecclestone.

Ecclestone's part-time motorcycle sales trading from the lab expanded quickly into an empire based in Bexleyheath, near his home in Kent, to rival the countrywide multi-million pound organization of motorbike legend Mike Hailwood's father, Stan. Deals in property yielded even more riches.

'By the time I was twenty-one I had car dealerships and motorcycle distributorships and then I started messing around with interests in property,' says Ecclestone, 'and one thing led to another. When you are in at that level of business you can't get out. It just seems to go on and on.

'I did a bit of racing on motorbikes at first when I was about fifteen, and I loved it. I was a bit of a charger and I was quite quick at one stage, but I fell off about twelve times and hurt myself every time. I woke in hospital once too often and thought, "This is crazy." I didn't want to spend the rest of my life in a wheelchair or looking up at a ceiling, so I quit in the 1950s to concentrate on my businesses. But later, because I was so hooked on racing and loved it so much and everything to do with it, I got back into racing. Only this time I switched to cars.'

In a cupboard in his office there is a book, dated 1951 but long out of print, that records Ecclestone's earliest car racing triumphs. One entry reads 'The Junior Brands Hatch Championship, 8 April 1951, an event limited to those drivers who had not won or come second in a final, was won by Bernard Ecclestone in the latest Cooper MK5/JAP at 62.03 mph.' Then it is recorded that in the Open Challenge at Brands Hatch on 12 May Heat One was 'a flyer won by Bernard Ecclestone at 66.05 mph,' and the *Daily Telegraph* Trophy Heat One was 'another flyer won by Ecclestone at 66.03 mph.'

In the big Brands Open Challenge Final in September 1951,

Bernie, in his Cooper-Norton, was in with a fine chance of victory. He swept to a win in his heat at 60.04 mph, just ahead of his good friend Stuart Lewis-Evans, who went on to become a Formula One racer but was tragically killed at the 1958 Morocco Grand Prix. The pages recall the dramatic events of the final: 'George Wicken stalled on the line. Andre Loens, Lewis-Evans, Whitehouse and Ecclestone stormed into Clearways. The second time round Loens led Whitehouse, Ecclestone, Leary, Lewis-Evans and Brandon. Third time round it was Ecclestone, Loens and Whitehouse first into Bottom Straight. Then Loens took to the grass, lost a wheel and skidded across the track in front of Ecclestone, Leary and Whitehouse. Ecclestone spun out to the right, his Cooper climbed up the safety banking, jumping onto a spectator's parked Riley car, unfortunately breaking a spectator's leg as a result. Whitehouse and Brandon took safety on the grass. Leary's car also took to the grass but rolled over on him and broke his collar bone. The race continued uninterrupted. St Johns gallant ambulance men and the mechanics cleared up.'

Bernie enjoys reminiscing about his days as a racer. 'They were great days with a lot of fun to be had and some smashing blokes to race against,' he says. 'I even tried to qualify for Monaco in a one-off effort … and failed miserably.

'When I was in a position later to mix my passion for racing with the chance to own my own Formula One team and I bought Brabham it was like having all my birthdays at the same time.'

'I couldn't get the feeling for racing out of my blood. I just loved it. Still do. My business was doing well but I couldn't keep away from racing and it was easy for me with that sort of feeling to get involved. I was a racer then and I still am now. My attitude these days is just as it was when I first came into Formula One: to try and make it better for everybody. Better for the public, better for the teams and better for the drivers. Everybody, in fact.'

Bernie claims that he never thinks about how he managed to rise from humble beginnings to the position in which he now finds himself. He says, 'I know how I did it, but I never think about it, not for a second. I don't ever look back. That would be bloody stupid. And, really, I am still doing the same sort of things I have always done, maybe on a slightly bigger scale. But so many things have given me great pleasure over the years. I don't think I'd change one single aspect of my life. If ever anything was bad it probably later on helped to make something good or better; I always think that nothing is all bad and I just look for the good.'

Having amassed a personal fortune as a businessmen and property developer in boom-time London and the home counties, Bernie's time was variously filled as a motorbike racer who frequently fell off, as a fiercely committed racing car driver, and as a team owner, who with Brabham, the team he bought in 1971, and driver Nelson Piquet, won world titles in 1981 and 1983. He withdrew from the championships in 1987 after his driver Elio de Angelis was killed in private practice at Le Castellet in the south of France and later sold the team to a Swiss financier who ended up in jail for massive frauds.

'The Brabham times were memorable in many ways,' admits Ecclestone, 'and winning a couple of titles was, of course, a tremendous achievement but once it was over and done with, and the team was sold, that was it. The episode was finished and there was no point in sitting on my laurels there were other things to do. Other mountains to climb. Different challenges.

'Even when we were winning everything, I was more often than not already on my way out of the circuit by helicopter heading home as my cars were crossing the line. People couldn't understand it, they couldn't figure out why I wasn't hanging around for the celebrations. But I had done my job and there were 500 more tasks waiting to be dealt with so what was the point in sticking around? What the hell more could I do? I'd have just been wasting my time when I could have been doing something more useful than waiting for people to pat me on the back. It's the same nowadays. I don't very often stay at the track once the race is underway. My part in the job has been accomplished, so I might as well get off home.'

A helicopter from the track to the nearest airport and then one of his two jets, one of them an eighty-seater, hangared at the wartime fighter base Biggin Hill, rushes him to England so that he can be back behind his desk by 8.30 a.m. on Monday morning. Or, if he needs the break and he is handily placed in a country adjoining Switzerland, he will fly to link up with his wife and two daughters at the ritzy hotel he bought in Gstaad, the centre of the universe for the winter jet-and-ski set.

Ecclestone almost quit Formula One when his dearest friend Jochen Rindt, the Austrian heart-throb, was killed practising for the Italian Grand Prix in 1970. 'Jochen and I were partners, we were friends and we were going to run a Formula One team together,' he says, 'and the sheer pleasure of working with him, his sense of humour and his feeling for fun which is sadly missing in drivers these days, made him a wonderful mate. When he was killed it was a terrible time for me and it was difficult to cope with the loss. I have been close to a lot of men who have unfortunately been killed, but Jochen's death was such a shock I can't describe it. It hit me so hard I kept away from racing for some time afterwards, and I nearly pulled out altogether because it was so difficult to take.'

Ecclestone was at Monza when the charismatic Rindt, well on his way to the 1970 championship, crashed during a practice session. Ecclestone burst through a cordon of police and marshals and ran along the track to where the wreckage of the Lotus was strewn, but by the time he had got there his friend had been pulled clear and was on his way to hospital. When Bernie eventually discovered Rindt's whereabouts and hurried to the clinic it was already too late. He was dead.

'When Ayrton Senna was killed at Imola,' says Ecclestone, 'it was a terribly bad feeling personally not quite the same as when Jochen was killed because I was much closer to him. In Senna's case I probably reacted in the same way as everybody else; it didn't seem possible for him to die in a race car. Anybody else, any other driver, yes, but not Ayrton. He had always seemed indestructible. It's a silly thing to say, isn't it? We all know racing is dangerous and guys do get hurt but Senna getting killed? That was out of the question. He was going to retire a very rich and successful man. It was total disbelief when I found out he was dead I was just numb. I suppose the one thing you can say is that when a driver gets killed while he's racing he at least goes out doing exactly what he wanted to do. In a way, I don't find that at all depressing. If

I die, which I probably will do one day, I hope it is doing something I enjoy doing.'

He quickly reverts to the theme that runs like a common thread throughout racing, an absence of overall sentimentality or any weakness for nostalgia in case, perhaps, he has to bare any part of his soul and expose the sort of inner feelings which are best kept private. Nobody in Formula One is keen to contemplate the that's it, sorry, but he's dead and gone, nothing we can do about it factor.

'We don't have a house full of memorabilia and not much more in the office and the only photographs we've got of any driver at home are of Senna,' he says, 'that's how highly I regarded him and what a friend I considered him to be. But, otherwise, I don't have tons of stuff to remind me of the past. It's tomorrow that counts.' Nevertheless Ecclestone was deeply wounded when the Senna family, out of a sad misunderstanding which has since been resolved, barred him from attending his friend's funeral in Brazil. He went to the country just the same and watched the ceremony on television in his hotel room.

Drivers, naturally, play a major role as the top-of-the-bill attractions in Ecclestone's touring spectacular which receives 27,000 television hours a year and is watched in more than 200 countries. His feelings for the drivers sway according to their levels of capability, their courage, their attitude and their appeal to him and the wider public, so much so that he has been known to boost a driver's retainer, to have him placed where Ecclestone wants. He made up a £3 million shortfall to buy out Nigel Mansell's IndyCar contract from the Newman-Haas team in order to bring the British hero back to Formula One to drive for

Williams in a four-race deal after two seasons in America. Mansell, in his turn, repaid the faith put in him by Ecclestone by amazingly winning the last race of the 1994 season in Australia after Schumacher had barged Damon Hill off the track in an explosive and controversial finale.

Generally, though, he feels drivers are paid far too much money. Once, when there was the hint of a strike among drivers who felt aggrieved at some pre-season conditions imposed on them, an irate Bernie told me: 'Thinking of going on strike are they? Bloody good. I'll just go along the Formula 3000 grid and tell all the guys there they are now Formula One drivers. Let's see how many of them turn the chance down. I'll tell you. None. And those buggers, those prima donnas, who go on strike will have plenty of time to sit on their private jets, count the zeroes and add up the figures on those great big fat contracts those who can read, that is and realize just how bloody lucky they are.'

He questions the massive amounts of money drivers demand and sometimes get saying, 'The thing is, none of them is worth the sort of money they are talking about these days. But I don't blame the drivers. If a guy is offered £20 million you can't really expect him to hold up his hands in protest and say "No, no, no, I couldn't possibly, I couldn't take it, it is far too much money." It is the constructors, the sponsors and the team owners who should be certified for offering that sort of money in the first place. OK, they sometimes get together and try to cap drivers' retainers and keep them to sensible levels, but in the end it usually falls apart because they argue they are in Formula One to win and they have got to have the best of everything, drivers included, to achieve their goal.'

He singles out Ferrari ace Michael Schumacher as the driver every team owner would sign, if only he could afford to buy the German genius's services. 'Michael is quite clearly the best,' says Bernie, 'he is head and shoulders above the rest. And, far from Enzo Ferrari's old idea that a married driver penalizes himself at least one second a lap because he is sub-consciously thinking about his responsibilities, Michael is worth more than a second a lap to any team. He is that much better than anybody else on the grid. In a full race he is worth thirty seconds over most of the other guys and that's because of his overtaking skill, the way he cuts so ruthlessly through anybody in his path and his intelligence and remarkable ability to be able to read and pace a race.

'To find even half a second's advantage in a car is difficult and it take some doing, but Michael seems to manage even more than that. He is, quite simply, brilliant. But there is no point in shelling out millions of pounds for him unless everything else is right, unless the entire package he needs to perform to his maximum is as good as his ambitions for it. If you have just one aspect missing from the package you are wasting the big money you have spent on him.

'There is no question that Michael is on another planet as a racer. There is him, then there's the rest of them on the grid. He has a magic, love him or hate him, that appeals to everybody right across the world. He wants to be a winner all the time. He only knows one way. It's his instinct and he would be the same whatever money was paid to him. The money he gets from Ferrari, how ever much it is, doesn't make him go any quicker or drive any harder. That comes from what is in him, not what is in his bank account. It is because of performers like him that so

210

many people right around the world want to watch Formula One. And the audience is going to get even bigger when we take the races to the Far East and Malaysia, say, and China comes into the action.

'When Formula One was first shown on television it was just long shots of the cars going round corners with no particular sensation of speed or of the control needed by the drivers. Now we have on-board cameras, drivers' eye views, split-screens, kerbside shots, all the drama and interviews in the pits and marvellous slow-motion shots and close-ups of the action wherever it is happening. That's all very fine but we also still need the great drivers, the characters who give the sport its heartbeat.

'That's why Gerhard Berger was so valuable. And it is a shame he quit. He was such a tremendous personality and a gem of a man whom I like very much. He was full of tricks and practical jokes. Men like him are a rare breed. Unfortunately they are few and far between. They are more than just drivers; they are wonderful people with something extra to offer. It is why Schumacher is such a superstar, he gives the public what they want 110 per cent effort all the time. And he is larger than reality. In years to come people will boast, like they do about Senna, that they saw him race.

'For totally different reasons Eddie Irvine fits into the category of drivers people want to see. I may have had my reservations about him when he first came into Formula One, but I see in him now a good guy who is a great character. He is serious enough about his racing, but he wants to have fun too. He is all right by me. The trouble is that he has been given, or made to have, a bad reputation. And he does not deserve it in my opinion. But he doesn't do anything to rectify the misconceptions about himself. In short, he doesn't give a stuff. If people say something bad about him and make a judgement he just shrugs and thinks "If that's your opinion, that's your opinion. Sod it." And he just gets on with his life. He couldn't care less.'

Irvine, the Ulsterman who earned worldwide notoriety after a debut grand prix punch-up with Ayrton Senna and further infamy with a series of crashes, once dismissed thirty-seven-year-old Damon Hill, a neighbour in Dublin, as a 'tired old man' after a racetrack showdown. His outspokenness has earned him a good few rebukes from many drivers, among them Hill, Johnny Herbert, Jacques Villeneuve and David Coulthard, in a series of clashes in his five-year Formula One career.

But his patient, some would argue subservient, role as a sacrificial and supportive number two albeit for a £3 million a year wage packet to Schumacher at Ferrari during the hard-fought championship years of 1997 and 1998 when the German had to master a wayward car and compensate with sheer skill for the car's deficiencies, earned this tribute from Ecclestone: 'If there was a prize for driver of the year I would give it to Irvine. He has been in 1998 in particular the perfect teammate for Michael. You could not ask for a guy to be more loyal to Ferrari and Schumacher. He has said openly that Schumacher is the best in the world, that he is happy to support him as a number two and that he would do everything in his power to help Michael win the championship. It is wonderful for Michael to have back-up like that.

'Ferrari are lucky to have such a combination working together so harmoniously and with the team's interests at heart.

But we shouldn't imagine for a second that Irvine is not his own man; he is a character, an individual. And, let's be honest, we need a few individuals in this game. We don't want stereotypes. I think there is a lot more to come from him and Formula One will benefit.'

Ecclestone has some strong opinions on the failure of Damon Hill, the 1994 champion who slid to virtual anonymity after being off-loaded so mysteriously by Frank Williams in his 1996 championship year, to negotiate a title-challenging drive with McLaren instead of chasing shadows with the Arrows team and then, to start with at least, at Jordan.

'I don't know how much Damon was offered, or what the deal was, and what he was offered by other people or whether he took into account that the McLaren offer was not enough,' he says. 'But it is a case of what you are trying to do with your life and your career. And when you are about to finish and your career is tailing off you are better to give yourself all the chances you can.

'You have to live on your reputation from then on in and, surely, it is far better and more preferable to live on a reputation that is high when you go out rather than on one that is low. People are more likely to remember you for winning two or three titles than just one. That gets forgotten too quickly. His future, when he eventually calls it a day and stops racing, depends on how good and successful he has been and what memories people have of him like his dad, Graham. It would have been much better for him if he could have packed it all in with two or three championships instead of just one. As it is he could easily be forgotten. That's sad because Damon's record of wins per race up to the time he left Williams was fantastic, it was its own testimony to his ability as a very clever, reliable and experienced driver. You don't lose that level of talent overnight and when he is on his game there are few who are better or who can be relied upon to get the car home.

'My feeling is that Damon might have gone to McLaren for about 20 per cent of what he got at Jordan and the car might not have been any good. Then he would have been in trouble. And, if you looked at Jordan's results from the year before, it appeared to be a car with a lot of potential. If you properly weigh up the whole situation as Damon no doubt did and say, well, the McLaren had a better look to it than the Jordan for winning races, but no guarantees, and there is a big difference in the money he was being offered by Eddie Jordan, he probably made the right decision at the time.

'I am convinced that if he had taken the chance and had accepted Ron Dennis's deal he would have more than doubled his earnings, and, I firmly believe, he would have been world champion again. He certainly has the talent and the ability. When you have won a world championship, and as many races as he has won, it is proof in itself that you are no mug.

'The problem Damon had in the early part of 1998 was that despite doing all those things and achieving so much he was not motivated. What's the point in charging round getting nowhere. Are you going to fight if you are seventh or eighth? Big deal. You make up a place. So what? People like Damon need to be motivated. It's the whole point. Unless he is in a team that offers him a good chance and a car that can win, provided he gives it his all, he is not going to be motivated. Maybe the package just wasn't good enough for him to win. But I just don't think he has given the best of himself. We may not have seen him on the podium, but we may have seen some better results from him.'

When I asked him to choose who would have formed his dream Formula One grid, the circuit the drivers would race and the car in which they would travel the notion appeals to Ecclestone.

'Ah, if only ...' he muses, 'wouldn't that be something? The ideal setting would be Monaco. Where else? People argue you can't overtake there, but that's bullshit. Any driver with the balls to do it can overtake anywhere. On any track. It's all about determination. Monaco has so much atmosphere, it just breathes excitement and anticipation. There is nowhere like it in the world, it is unique. It may be the slowest grand prix of them all, but it is still dodgy with all those barriers bang up against the track and no run-offs and for two hours or more it demands a level of intense concentration and precision from the drivers that is unparalleled on any other track in the sport.

'To race for all you are worth in Monte Carlo needs a special commitment, a driver has to be at ten tenths of his ability and the car has to be nimble, reliable and powerful and up for the job. So I would put the drivers all in a Renault-Williams as it was when it was a world beater in the early 1990s. They would all start equal and only be separated by their ability and determination.

'I love daring drivers, real racers, chargers who given the smallest opening will go for it and give their all to win. That's why I would have Nigel Mansell in pole position. He had all those ingredients and he would be full value. He would guarantee it would be one hell of a race because there wasn't a driver around who didn't get pleasure at the very thought of beating Mansell and they would have to get through him to take the lead. Not an easy job as so many guys found out when they tried it on. He, just like the others I will pick, would show that you certainly can overtake in Monaco. And most of them could do it three or four times a lap. Generally these days drivers have got it in their heads they can't, either because somebody has told them, or they don't believe themselves that it can be done unless the car in front of them pulls over.

'Mansell on pole, then Ayrton Senna alongside, with Michael Schumacher next in line. Jochen Rindt would line up fourth. Then it would be Ronnie Peterson, Alain Prost, Alan Jones, followed by Jackie Stewart and Niki Lauda, James Hunt, Graham Hill, Fangio and Nelson Piquet.

'I would place all the out-and-out chargers on the front few rows with the clever, intelligent delivery boys like Prost and Stewart ready to pick up the pieces, and maybe win, after the almost inevitable crash among the front runners, the dynamic guys who wouldn't take a step backwards how ever severe the challenge or yield an inch of ground.

'When it comes down to a judgement on who rates as the absolute master I would choose Senna every time. He was unbeatable in Monaco and won there a record six times, five times in a McLaren, which was a tribute to the accuracy of his driving and his remarkable and uncanny ability to cope with the intense pressure a place like that can impose. He had everything. He was able to concentrate fully for the entire race. That's a problem a lot of other drivers cannot overcome. And it didn't make any difference how tough it was, how hard he had to race or whatever the conditions. It was all the same to him. He was a genius everywhere he drove. He only knew one way to perform flat out. But he was clever enough to understand where his limit was, as good as he knew he was, and not to cross it.

'He was also very hard on himself and the car and he was quite ruthless in getting the best out of the equipment when it wasn't so good. He carried McLaren for a long time when the car wasn't so hot and he showed that he could handle all the pressure, how ever intense it was, and all the difficulties that can present themselves to a driver with his responsibilities. For me, he was a forceful but flawless driver. On top of all that I liked him very much indeed, we were good pals, and I found him to be a charming guy and great company.'

Bernie adds, 'It is impossible to leapfrog the years and value for their talent a top ten list of the greatest drivers because the different decades demanded different techniques, but the inescapable fact is that drivers of skill, whatever age they lived in, stood out from the mere mortals. And you can only imagine just what a thriller of a race it would be if by some miracle of magic you could spirit all these guys onto a Monaco grid and flag them off for seventy-eight laps.

'They were all the sort of guys who just got on with the programme, men who made their best efforts to get the car home. Mansell, for instance, always gave you the impression that if it all went wrong and the car stopped and he was near enough to the finish he'd pick it up and carry it on his back across the line if he thought he had the remotest chance of winning.

'Guys like Prost and Stewart, both deep thinkers about racing and the way to do it as safely as they could, did the business as slowly as they dared without unnecessarily sticking their necks out to win every time. Their aim and they never tried to disguise the fact that they weren't there to break records for the sake of it was to win the championship at the slowest, safest possible speed and to get the points. They worked on the principle that if you don't finish you can't win titles and they were never embarrassed to finish third or fourth and not be a winner just so long as they had achieved their target of scoring points.

'You could never claim that Prost or Stewart were exciting drivers not like James Hunt. He was pure magic, everybody's idea of what a racing driver should be daring, colourful and full of fun. A real character. The problem was with James that you never knew, and neither, I suspect did he for most of the time, what the hell he was going to do in a race. It all seemed to hang and depend on his mood. But he was a thrilling driver when he was going for it.

'What about Nigel Mansell? What a driver, especially in Monaco. He revelled in the place. He was the sort of driver who could only give of his best. People identified with him. I think they saw themselves in Nigel because he didn't put anything on, he had no airs and graces. And everybody wanted him to be world champion. He had that certain something, a popular appeal, quality that people all over the world seemed to admire. He was a moaner at times, a right whinger, but even that was done with what he believed was a genuine sense of grievance and with justification. You could never fault him for his sincerity. He was tremendous behind the wheel, a giant of a driver and one heck of a man to try and beat. He would never quit or lose heart. He would race down pit lane, out of the garage, on the track and everywhere else if he thought he could be a winner. I was sorry when we lost him for a while to IndyCars and was happy to play my own small part in bringing him back to Formula One where he really belonged all the time.' Bernie's 'small part' was to spend hours on end on the telephone talking to Mansell in Florida and team owner Carl Haas in Chicago, fire up the interest of his old boss Frank Williams who had split with him in awkward circumstances, buy out the Mansell contract from Newman-Haas and persuade the self-willed Brummie that he could rekindle his Formula One career if he abandoned his £15 million shoreside estate on the Gulf of Mexico and gave grands prix another go. All of which he did.

Ecclestone's appreciation of Schumacher's quality as a ready-made replacement for Senna inspired him to include him in his line-up of all-time greats. 'Schumacher is the genius of his day,' says Bernie. 'After Senna was killed he inherited the mantle of the finest driver of his generation. Rightly so. He is both clever and quick and that is an unbeatable combination when you align it with a car that can do the business. At both Benetton and Ferrari he made the difference between success and failure and no other drivers I know had the ability to do that. His worth to any team and that's why so many wanted him is immeasurable.'

The other drivers on Bernie's dream grid merited their choice either by their appeal to him as full-blooded racers or because of their timeless quality as men who had the ability to make a car do what they wanted and to tame tracks, how ever difficult the weather conditions, in a way that set them apart from the rest.

Rindt, the only posthumous world champion, had contested

only sixty GPs with six wins, when he was killed at Monza in 1970. Swedish ace Ronnie Peterson, another absolute flyer of a driver, and regarded as one of the quickest and most spectacular of all time, was twice the runner-up in the championship, and won ten of his 123 GPs. He also perished in a crash at the Italian Grand Prix, in 1978 when he was just thirty-four years old. Alan Jones, a burly Australian tough guy with a fearsome competitive spirit, put the Williams team on the grand prix roll of honour by earning them their first world title in 1980. Stewart, the shrewd Scot who later became a team owner, was a pioneer of safety in Formula One. He was three times world champion although he only competed in ninety-nine GPs. Aside from his titles in 1969, 1971 and 1973, he was runner-up in 1968 and 1972 and finished third in 1965, his first year in the top flight. And he never once spilled blood or broke a bone.

Prost, nicknamed 'The Professor' because of his cerebral approach to racing, won four world titles in 199 GPs, achieving a record fifty-one victories. Niki Lauda, another Austrian, lived to race again after a scarring fireball crash that nearly cost him his life at the infamous Nurburgring in Germany in 1976. He awoke to hear a priest given him the last rites.

Hunt, the archetypal British hero and a product of the public school system, was crowned Formula One king in 1976 when Lauda pulled out of the Japanese Grand Prix in a treacherous downpour at Suzuka but never again closed in on the championship. He was a spectacular hard charger in the Ecclestone mould and won ten times from ninety-two grands prix. But he had seventeen crashes in six years.

Graham Hill was known as 'Mr Monaco' after winning five

times in the principality. He also won two world championships and had fourteen GP victories. Nelson Piquet, the cocky Brazilian infamous for his bitter personal disputes that put Nigel Mansell in a rage when they were both at Williams, had an arrogance and self-belief that angered rivals and associates alike but it was central to his style and was welcomed by his race team bosses who could count on his confidence to get the car to the line. He won two titles, forty-four races and was on pole twenty-four times.

Juan Manuel Fangio, who died in 1995, contested only fifty-one grands prix, driving for Alfa Romeo, Maserati, Mercedes and Ferrari, but he dwells in the archives, and the memory banks of the students of racing, as one of the greatest drivers in history. The Argentine maestro, a glorious winner when 160 mph cars wanted to misbehave and slew sideways on tyres that were not much wider than the wheels on supermarket trolleys, and steered just about as accurately, won the world championship a record-setting five times, the last one in 1957.

Ecclestone is at his most content when he is dealing with Formula One and its interests and development, how ever complex or difficult the agenda, and his devotion in both time and energy to that end is signified by the long hours he works, either in his office or overseas. When other diverting factors that demand his attention or upset his equilibrium come into play, particularly concerning his motives or his reputation or his family Ecclestone can be famously prickly and as ferociously defensive as any cornered animal. Despite all his achievements, in business and sport, when asked what is his greatest treasure Ecclestone's reply is immediate and succinct: 'My family.'

Two incidents, both of which became long-running sagas between 1997 and 1998 served to indicate just how deeply he feels when outsiders believe he is too hardened, too rich, too lofty a celebrity, too important and too world weary to care.

The situations ran parallel in what for Ecclestone must have been the most trying twelve months of his life. One concerned hurtful and damaging accusations that his spectacular 6 ft 2 in wife Slavica, a former model, had been a honey-trap spy, a bedroom agent, for the Croatian Secret Services before she and Bernie had met and married in 1985.

The second put Ecclestone at the centre of a political storm when it was revealed that he had made a £1 million donation, the biggest ever, to New Labour and they later did a U-turn on their intentions to ban tobacco advertising in Formula One. Both situations drew a focus on both Bernie and his loved ones. They angered, puzzled and hurt a man who was motivated by defence of his wife's and family honour on one hand and, he still insists, a genuine a desire to be a benefactor to what he deemed to be a worthy and deserving political cause, without an ulterior motive, on the other.

In the case of his wife, a former boyfriend of Slavica's, Momir Blagojevic, made the spy claims about her and these were published alongside nude photographs of her, taken when she was a struggling and naive young model, in the weekly magazine *Imperijal* in November 1997.

Slavica was so disturbed and traumatized by the claims, apparently published without verification by a twenty-three-year-old journalist, that she had to have counselling. Ecclestone's fury at the slur, exacerbated by his wife's upset, fired him to relentlessly pursue the criminal libel through the courts. The offenders flirted with contempt and frequently failed to show up for the hearings in the Croatian capital Zagreb, despite warrants being issued for their arrest. Ecclestone's rage increased in direct proportion to the futility and helplessness he felt at the failure of proper justice.

It took six court hearings Slavica and Bernie attended five of them before Blagojevic, a former district attorney in the seaside town of Rijeka, and journalist Roko Vuletic finally appeared. They both apologized abjectly. Blagojevic confessed that nothing he had said was true and he had been under emotional pressure when he made his accusation to the magazine. Vuletic admitted he had not checked the veracity of his information and said, 'I am really sorry for the consequences and I apologize to Mrs Ecclestone.'

The matter did not end there in typical fashion Ecclestone ruthlessly pursued a second claim for damages he knew would cripple the paper. That was settled in mid-summer, four months after the initial apology, and was one of the biggest settlements for damages ever awarded in Croatia. All the money was donated by Slavica to an orphanage.

Afterwards Ecclestone said, 'I would fight to my last breath in defence of my family and my wife's good name. She didn't deserve to have all that rubbish thrown at her and those guys could have withdrawn it at any time. But they didn't, they kept it going. And that's what upset me. They knew it was just a pack of lies and I wasn't going to let them get away with that sort of slur no matter how much time or money it cost. It only mattered to me that those I love should always be protected.'

Good friend … bad enemy.

The political hot potato of the £1 million donation that Bernie gave to New Labour, long before they were elected to govern, had far less of a sinister or compromising motive than was widely believed or understood despite the mileage made out of it by scandal-mongering MPs with an eye for a chance for a splash of Commons limelight.

When the rumpus broke Ecclestone was only too happy to clear up misunderstandings which were gathering dangerous momentum every time an ill-informed minister or MP opened his mouth or yet another Bernie basher wanted to jump on the band-wagon.

He explained, 'I made the donation purely and simply because I liked Tony Blair and all that he seemed to stand for. We had met only once, at the British Grand Prix at Silverstone in 1996, and I got on with him. I thought then that he was an extremely capable young guy who was determined to take Britain in the right direction. He was on the same track as me. I was only with him and his wife for about half an hour, but it was long enough for me to be impressed by him and to realize he was a winner.

'And when the Tories embarked on that dreadful "Devil Eyes" poster campaign against him in the election run-up I was disgusted. I thought that smacked of dirty tactics. It was well below the belt. And I thought they were knocking the guy unfairly and portraying him in the wrong light altogether.

'I hadn't a clue then what I might do to help, or even if I wanted to do anything at all, until a friend who is not, repeat categorically not, a member of the Labour Party, but a supporter, asked me if I'd like to make a donation. I thought about it for a while. I thought about Blair, remembered how much I liked him and his ideas and New Labour and their ambitions for the country without giving way to the unions. And I reasoned, "Well, I am a big, big tax payer and I bring a lot of money and work into this country." I love the old place. It is where I want to live because I am British through and through. I could easily run my business from elsewhere in the world, but I don't, I run it from London. It is what I most enjoy and get satisfaction from. Britain is a lovely place to be. And I want to see it and everyone who lives here prosper and be happy. The last thing I want to see is a government in the hands or under the undue influence of the unions. A fair balance would have to include the business sector, too.

'And that's why, because I did not want to see the party totally dependent on union money, I got my accountant to draw up a company cheque for £1 million against my director's loan account. He posted it off and I didn't even have to sign it myself.'

Disclosure of the donation stirred the political pot and the tobacco advertising issue was thrown in as the main ingredient. But Ecclestone insisted, 'It was all done and completed long before this stupid tobacco ban issue came out. I gave the money simply because I wanted to. No strings. No expectations. No promises wanted or even asked for me or Formula One. No benefits. I had no motives at all. I wasn't thinking about getting anything in return, not a knighthood, the freedom of Kensington, a statue of me in Hyde Park, an OBE, or even a bloody bus pass. I am not a beggar looking for a handout. I have never asked for anything on my life. I'm not like some other prominent so-called tycoons with a few bob who want to buy honours and creep around people who can give them peerages, a bit of status and God knows what else.

'I've got a drawerful of letters from people who all want to give me or recommend me for some medal or decoration and I have turned them all down. I have all the honours I need from right around the world. They have been awarded by leaders of countries who feel I have brought them benefits and I feel privileged and proud to have been presented with them because they are for my efforts and work in Formula One and not my money.'

He continued, 'What is important to remember is this: for me to make a £1 million contribution to New Labour when they were running for election and might not get in, and still expect guarantees of something in return, would be sheer lunacy. That would be like being in a casino and throwing a ball on a roulette wheel that didn't have any numbers. You just wouldn't take such a mad gamble if you wanted a return for your money. I may not be the brightest guy in the world, but I am not the dumbest idiot either and for me to make a contribution in January when they were campaigning and might not even get the votes, thinking and planning that I was going get something back or obligate them, is a non-runner. Anyway, knowing politicians as I do, they might not even have kept to their promise. And I am not that big or stupid a gambler. The simple truth was, I could afford the million quid and it seemed right to give it to a cause that was going to keep the unions in check under the authority of Blair, a man whose ideas I admired and supported. What's wrong with that?

'My father was a Tory but when I was growing up I didn't have a thought in my head about politics, anymore than I do nowadays. I couldn't give a damn who is in power just so long as they are doing the right things and what I consider to be the best for the country.'

Rumours circulated in Westminster that Ecclestone had funded the Tory party to the tune of some £14 million. He responds to this suggestion by *laughing and saying, 'What a joke. It is all fiction. I never gave them a pen*ny. Where do these figures come from? I'd love somebody from the Conservative Party to come to see me and confirm that I had donated £14 million to them because I would like it all back please. Then I really would be in a win-win-win situation.

'All the talk about sleaze was complete rubbish. It was typically political claptrap dreamed up by somebody, God knows who, to make mischief for Blair and me and to attach something to us that just was not there. The truth is that when I met him at Number Ten in October to talk about the exemption, I'd had no conversation with anybody in New Labour about the issue. None at all. Not a word. And, anyway, when we were in Downing Street it was Max Mosley who did most of the talking. Not me.'

The controversial cheque hovered somewhere between New Labour Party HQ and Ecclestone's Knightsbridge office before it was finally returned six months later with Bernie saying, 'I didn't really want it back. And I certainly didn't expect any favours for sanctioning it in the first place. It has all been too silly for words. But given the right circumstances and no bloody fuss I would do exactly the same thing again and I would expect precisely the same return for my money. Nothing.'

Begging letters and suggestions galore about the gift flooded Ecclestone's offices as the figure of £1 million moved into currency slang as a 'Bernie', alongside such euphemisms as a 'monkey' and a 'pony'.

When the fuss had died down and the politicians had exhausted their rhetoric and returned to their pastime of abusing each other instead Bernie said, 'You have to laugh don't you? Bloody politicians will grab at anything they think might pull them along. Truth is, I don't have any allegiances at all. Not to a party. Not to any particular politician. And who's to say that in a few years I might be of the opinion that the Tories are making a better job running the country and I will give them £1 million or £2 million quid to help them out.'

Good friend … bad enemy.